PERSIAN GULF STATES

KUWAIT, QATAR, BAHRAIN, OMAN, AND THE UNITED ARAB EMIRATES

MIDDLE EAST
REGION IN TRANSITION

PERSIAN GULF STATES
KUWAIT, QATAR, BAHRAIN, OMAN, AND THE UNITED ARAB EMIRATES

EDITED BY LAURA S. ETHEREDGE, ASSOCIATE EDITOR, MIDDLE EAST GEOGRAPHY

Britannica® Educational Publishing
IN ASSOCIATION WITH
ROSEN
EDUCATIONAL SERVICES

Published in 2011 by Britannica Educational Publishing
(a trademark of Encyclopædia Britannica, Inc.)
in association with Rosen Educational Services, LLC
29 East 21st Street, New York, NY 10010.

Distributed exclusively by Rosen Educational Services.
For a listing of additional Britannica Educational Publishing titles, call toll free (800) 237-9932.

First Edition

Britannica Educational Publishing
Michael I. Levy: Executive Editor
J.E. Luebering: Senior Manager
Marilyn L. Barton: Senior Coordinator, Production Control
Steven Bosco: Director, Editorial Technologies
Lisa S. Braucher: Senior Producer and Data Editor
Yvette Charboneau: Senior Copy Editor
Kathy Nakamura: Manager, Media Acquisition
Laura S. Etheredge: Associate Editor, Middle East Geography

Rosen Educational Services
Alexandra Hanson-Harding: Editor
Nelson Sá: Art Director
Cindy Reiman: Photography Manager
Matthew Cauli: Designer, Cover Design
Introduction by Monique Vescia

Library of Congress Cataloging-in-Publication Data
Persian Gulf states: Kuwait, Qatar, Bahrain, Oman, and the United Arab Emirates/
edited by Laura S. Etheredge. — 1st ed.
p. cm. — (Middle East: region in transition)
"In association with Britannica Educational Publishing, Rosen Educational Services."
Includes bibliographical references and index.
ISBN 978-1-61530-327-4 (library binding)
1. Persian Gulf States—Encyclopedias. I. Etheredge, Laura.
DS247.A13P48 2011
953.6—dc22

2010034558

Manufactured in the United States of America

On the cover (clockwise from top left): The Sultan Qaboos Grand Mosque at night, near Muscat, Oman; Kuwait city, Kuwait at night; the financial center of Manama, Bahrain; Doha, Qatar, skyline seen from the bay at sunset. *Shutterstock.com.*

On pages 1, 9, 14, 18, 23, 28, 37, 44, 48, 52, 60, 70, 77, 81, 86, 93, 99, 104, 108, 112, 115, 123, 132, 136, 142, 149, 151, 155: This map of the Middle East focuses on five of the countries of the Persian Gulf—Kuwait, Qatar, Bahrain, Oman, and the United Arab Emirates. *NIMA. Courtesy of the University of Texas Libraries, The University of Texas at Austin*

CONTENTS

26

29

35

49

56

62

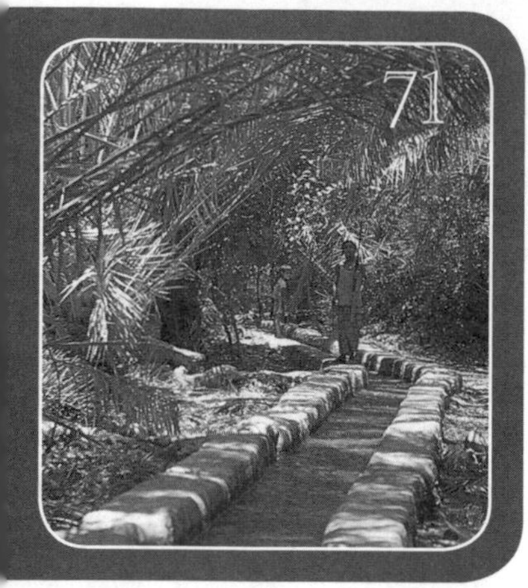
71

79

82

88

96

100

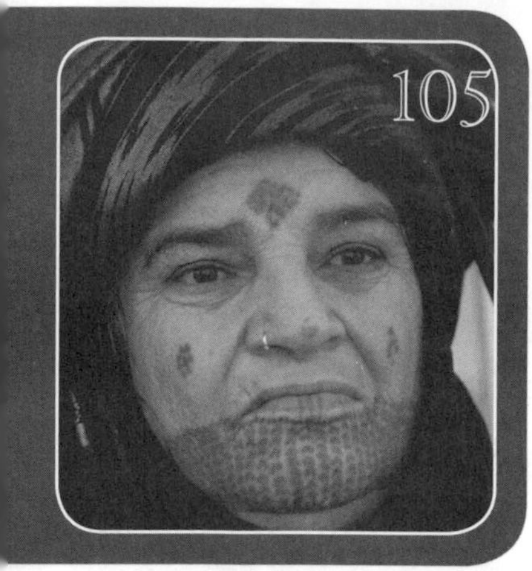
105

114

120

135

138

143

INTRODUCTION

Situated between the eastern Arabian Peninsula and southwestern Iran, the Persian Gulf has for centuries served as an important avenue for travel and trade. The five Persian Gulf states that form the subject of this volume—Oman, Kuwait, Qatar, Bahrain, and the United Arab Emirates—have distinct histories and characters yet share many fundamental similarities. With the exception of Oman, all five are relatively small, geographically speaking. Here, rich cultures managed to take root and to thrive in arid lands with limited or no sources of fresh water, where daytime temperatures in summer can sometimes reach a scorching 130 °F, and where the *shamāl* winds whip the desert sands into dramatic sandstorms. The harsh climate limits the possibilities for large-scale agriculture, so in many cases, food and food products are among the necessities that must be imported.

A shared Arab and Muslim heritage likewise binds the states of the Persian Gulf region. The slender minarets of mosques, silhouetted against the sky, are a common sight in the region, where religion permeates many aspects of daily life. From high in each tower, the call of the muezzin drifts over cities and villages, summoning the faithful to prayer five times a day. Sunni Muslims predominate in all the Arab states of the Persian Gulf region except in Oman, where Ibāḍī Muslims are in the majority, and in Bahrain, where Shīʿite Muslims are the largest religious group. The other gulf states have significant populations of Shīʿite Muslims as well.

Conservative Islamic culture has long had separate social practices for men and women. In many cases,

A man looks on as a vendor weighs out some grain in downtown Kuwait city, Kuwait, in November 2003. Yasser Al-Zayyat/AFP/Getty Images

modesty standards have customarily dictated that women veil themselves, though these customs are, in general, more relaxed in the Arab countries of the Persian Gulf region. As the region has become more modernized, women have won many rights and privileges, such as the right to vote and the right to hold political office, that once belonged exclusively to men.

Tribal relationships have long played a central role in the region, and in modern times, the tribe is the foundation upon which political rule has been most commonly built. The Arab states of the Persian Gulf region are chiefly ruled by monarchies where sons succeed fathers to the throne, sometimes by force. Political participation in the region, although relatively limited, has been on the increase.

The discovery of vast reserves of oil, beginning in the 1930s, radically transformed the economies of the Persian Gulf states. Traditional industries gave way to oil fields and refineries, although foreign interests owned and managed the oil industry in parts of the Persian Gulf until the 1970s, by which time most of these countries had gained their independence. Transformed by petroleum-driven income, the wealthy gulf states are now home to developments of global significance—such as the United Arab Emirates' Burj Khalifa, the world's tallest building—and, in some cases, some of the highest per capita incomes in the world. The governments of these states are thus able to house, educate, and provide free health care for their native populations, although foreign workers, many of whom are employed in industries such as construction, are barred from citizenship and its benefits. Male foreign workers make up a significant proportion of the gulf states' populations, and men easily outnumber women in most of these countries as a result.

More recently, the development of natural gas reserves has further enriched the region. The gulf states still rely heavily on income derived from the sale of energy resources, although many have made efforts to diversify their economies. One country that has successfully developed a multifaceted economy is the Kingdom of Bahrain, an effort that has been spurred in particular by the country's relatively small petroleum reserves. Bahrain is home to Aluminum Bahrain BSC, one of the world's largest aluminium smelters, and aluminum refining has become an important industry. The Bahraini economy is also tied to light manufacturing, ship repair, and financial services.

Against the backdrop of the ultra-modern capital city of Manama—one of the most important commercial and financial centres of the region—traditional dhows still ply the harbour. More religiously and ethnically diverse than many of its neighbours, Bahrain has begun promoting itself as a tourist destination, both for its warm climate and scenic seaside location and its historical richness.

Qatar is another gulf state with its sights focused on the future. The economy of this small desert peninsula was once based on fishing, trade, and pearling, although the export of pearls faltered once the Japanese introduced cultured pearls into the market during the 1920s. The subsequent development of oil fields brought in much-needed profits, and although Qatar possesses modest oil reserves relative to some of its more petroleum-rich neighbours, the country's oil-derived income nevertheless dominates its economy. By the 1970s its population, once one of the poorest in the world, boasted one of the world's highest per capita incomes.

In 1995 a bloodless coup saw the overthrow of the Qatari emir by his son, Sheikh Ḥamad ibn Khalīfah Āl Thānī. The current Qatari government—led by Sheikh

Ḥamad—has demonstrated a cautious commitment to creating a more politically open society and has placed a priority on developing its educational infrastructure. In Education City, a sprawling complex on the outskirts of the capital city of Doha, students attend branches of several prestigious American universities, including Carnegie Mellon University, Northwestern University, and Georgetown University. The popular satellite television network Al-Jazeera, founded in 1996 by Sheikh Ḥamad, is well known in the West.

The discovery of oil in Oman in 1964 drastically altered the fortunes of that country as well. Oman was isolated for decades by its sultan, Saʿīd ibn Taymūr, until he was overthrown by his son Qaboos—with the clandestine support of the British government—in 1970. Aided by the country's oil wealth, the new ruler embarked on a mission to modernize the country. Oman's distinctive culture remains very much apparent in its historical riches, including 17th century forts that once guarded the capital city of Muscat, the prehistoric settlements at Bāt, Al-Khutm, and Al-ʿAyn, and the Frankincense Trail, which is made up of stops along the ancient trade route. Some of the traditional sports of the Persian Gulf region, such as falconry and camel racing, continue to be practiced in the country as well.

The United Arab Emirates is a federation of emirates strategically located on the Arabian Peninsula. Abu Dhabi, the largest by far of the emirates, is the centre of the country's oil industry and contains the federation's capital city. The commercial and financial hub of the United Arab Emirates is the port city of Dubai, which also serves as the capital of the emirate of the same name. Wealth from oil revenues transformed Abu Dhabi in particular practically overnight, although not all the emirates in the federation were similarly fortunate, and those without the benefit of massive oil reserves—such as ʿAjmān and Umm al-Qaywayn—have had to harness their development to other industries and initiatives.

In addition to the discovery of oil, another important event that helped shape the modern politics of the region was the Iran-Iraq War (1980–88). The Iran-Iraq War followed on the heels of Iran's Islamic Revolution, which, in the late 1970s, saw the declaration of Iran as an Islamic republic led by Ayatollah Ruhollah Khomeini. One of the chief principles of the revolution was its export to other countries, a notion that threatened the stability of Iran's Persian Gulf neighbours. To defend against the Iranian threat as well as to promote cooperation on economic matters, in May 1981 the countries of Oman, Kuwait, Qatar, Bahrain, and the United Arab Emirates, along with Saudi Arabia, banded together to form the Gulf Cooperation Council.

The decade-long Iran-Iraq War also helped set the stage for the Persian Gulf War (1990–91). The conflict centred global attention on Kuwait, a small, wedge-shaped state on the Arabian Peninsula, when it was invaded and occupied by the neighbouring country of Iraq in August 1990. Ṣaddām Ḥussein, the Iraqi president, hoped to expand Iraq's power in the region and to seize control of Kuwait's oil reserves. International reaction was swift, and within six months a coalition of international forces, led by the United States, had driven the Iraqi forces out of Kuwait. The Iraqis had already damaged and looted many of the most important museums in the country, though, and the retreating Iraqi forces set fire to Kuwait's oil fields, which burned for months, cloaking the region in poisonous smoke. Substantial environmental damage was also done to the desert ecosystem by tanks and other pieces of military equipment as they rumbled across the desert.

More than a decade later, Kuwait has largely recovered from its war wounds. Like their neighbours elsewhere in the region, Kuwaiti citizens enjoy free health care, excellent education, subsidized housing, and, on average, one of the world's highest incomes per capita. While nearly all of the country's economy is still based on oil production, in 2009 the Kuwaiti government passed an economic development plan that commits the country to economic diversification.

Strategic locations and plentiful energy resources have enriched the gulf states and bolstered their economies, allowing their citizens to raise dazzling towers from the desert sands—but not without a cost. One pressing social problem is what to do about the large disenfranchised populations of expatriate workers who help these countries meet their economic goals. With small native populations, the gulf states have had to seek labour elsewhere. Many expatriates have settled in the region and have raised their children there, although they have not been granted many social rights—they cannot vote or organize into unions, and they risk deportation at any time. Another repercussion of an economy built on oil is the environmental cost. Growing oil pollution in the gulf crippled the fishing and shrimp industry in the region and threatens to impact tourism if beaches, scuba diving sites, and bird sanctuaries become fouled.

Worldwide economic woes and the international banking crisis at the end of the first decade of the 21st century did not leave the Persian Gulf states unscathed. Dubai, with its renowned focus on large-scale construction and real estate development, was hit hard by the crisis. Bahrain and Kuwait also experienced slower economic growth. As the world works to reduce its dependence on oil and new sources of alternative energy continue to be developed, these changes will also surely impact countries whose economies are fueled by petroleum. Today, though, the Persian Gulf states continue to thrive as their leaders increasingly embrace globalization, invest in education, and gradually work to create more open societies and more diverse economies than ever before—while remaining faithful to their Arab and Islamic heritage and traditions.

CHAPTER 1

Bahrain: The Land and Its People

Bahrain's total land area is slightly greater than that of Singapore. Saudi Arabia lies to the west across the Gulf of Bahrain, while the Qatar peninsula lies to the east. The King Fahd Causeway, 15 miles (24 km) long, links Bahrain to Saudi Arabia.

The state consists of two separate groups of islands, which together extend about 30 miles (50 km) from north to south and 10 miles (16 km) from east to west. The island of Bahrain accounts for seven-eighths of the country's total land area and is surrounded by smaller islands. Two of these—Al-Muḥarraq and Sitrah, both to the northeast—are joined to Bahrain Island by causeways that have facilitated residential and industrial development. An oil port, Sitrah handles not only the entire petroleum production of Bahrain but is also an export centre for oil fields in northeastern Saudi Arabia. Other islands in the group are Nabī Ṣāliḥ, Al-Muḥammadiyyah (Umm al-Ṣabbān), Umm

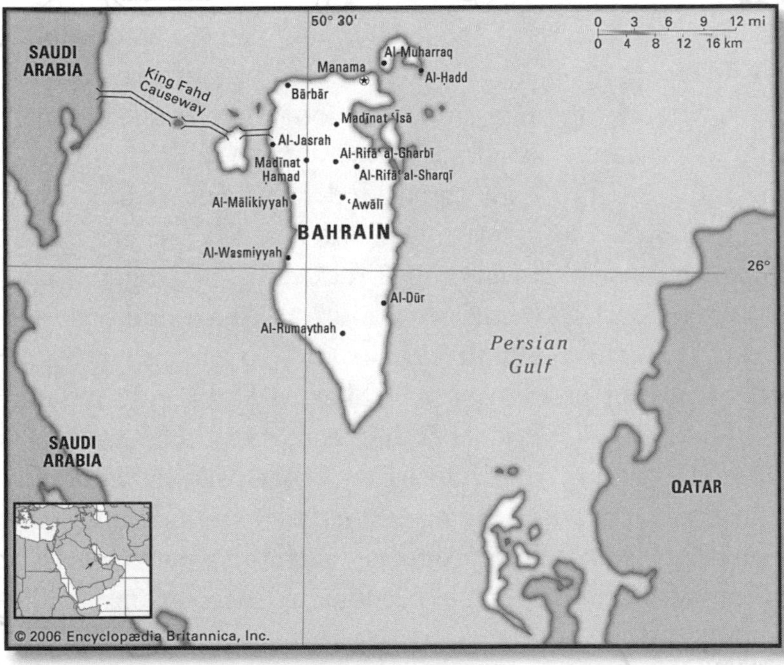

al-Naʿsān (linked by the King Fahd Causeway), and Jiddah. The second group consists of the Ḥawār Islands, which are situated near the coast of Qatar, about 12 miles (19 km) southeast of Bahrain Island; a dispute with Qatar over ownership of the islands was resolved in 2001, when the International Court of Justice awarded them to Bahrain. Small and rocky, they are inhabited by only a few fishermen and quarry workers, but they are believed to hold petroleum and natural gas reserves.

The majority of the population of Bahrain is Arab. Although most of the people are native-born Bahraini Arabs, there are also Arabs of Palestinian, Omani, and Saudi ancestry. Substantial foreign-born communities are also found in Bahrain; these residents hail from countries that include Iran, India, Pakistan, Britain, and the United States, and they account for more than one-third of the country's total population.

RELIEF AND DRAINAGE

While the small islands in both groups are rocky and low-lying, rising only a few feet above sea level, the main island is more varied in appearance. Geologically, the island consists of gently folded layers of sedimentary rocks: limestones, sandstones, and marls (loose clay, sand, or silt) formed during the Cretaceous, Paleogene, and Neogene periods (i.e., from about 145 to 2.6 million years ago). The central region is rocky and barren, rising to 440 feet (134 metres) above sea level at Al-Dukhān Hill (Jabal Al-Dukhān), the country's highest point. The southern and western lowlands consist of a bleak sandy plain with some salt marshes, while the northern and northwestern coasts afford a striking contrast, forming a narrow belt of date palms and vegetable gardens irrigated from prolific

Al-Muḥarraq

Al-Muḥarraq is a municipality in the state and emirate of Bahrain, on Al-Muḥarraq Island, the northernmost island of the Bahrain archipelago, in the Persian Gulf. It lies at the southwest tip of the island and is connected by a causeway, about 1.5 miles (2.5 km) long, to the capital city of Manama, on Bahrain Island. Many of its residents commute to work on the main island across the causeway.

Taken by the Portuguese (1521) and the Persians (1602), Al-Muḥarraq passed to the control of the Āl Khalīfah dynasty in 1783 with the rest of Bahrain. It developed as a trade centre, its harbour being the chief headquarters for the formerly important Bahraini pearl-diving industry, virtually extinct since the 1930s. At the beginning of the 20th century, Al-Muḥarraq's population was estimated at 20,000, and almost 300 pearling boats were harboured there. It was also politically important since the ruling sheikh used to reside there most of the year. Al-Muḥarraq has retained its character as a Middle Eastern town, with narrow, winding streets and traditional Arab souks (marketplaces).

Roughly horseshoe-shaped, Al-Muḥarraq Island is indented by Muḥarraq Bay on the south. Bahrain International Airport lies just north of Al-Muḥarraq city. Until shortly before Bahraini independence (1971), the air-field served as a Royal Air Force base, the country then being a British-protected state. Al-Ḥadd, another sizable town on the island, is on a spit at its southeast tip. South of Al-Ḥadd on a man-made island at the end of a 7-mile-long causeway is a shipbuilding yard and drydock financed by the Organization of Arab Petroleum Exporting Countries (OAPEC). The drydock opened in 1977 and is capable of accepting tankers of 450,000 deadweight tons. On a peninsula across the bay to the east of Al-Muḥarraq city are the village and fort of ʿArād; the fort was built by the Omanis during the brief (1799–1809) occupation of the country by the sultanate of Muscat and Oman.

springs and wells that tap artesian water. The source of this water is precipitation on the western mountains of Saudi Arabia, which flows into deep underground aquifers. The abundance of fresh water has provided Bahrain with fertile land, from which it gained importance historically as a harbour and trading centre in the Persian Gulf. Economic developments and population growth have outstripped the available artesian water in the country, and some three-fifths of the water used now comes from seawater desalinization plants powered by natural gas.

CLIMATE

Summer in Bahrain is unpleasant, as high temperatures frequently coincide with high humidity. Midday temperatures from May to October exceed 90 °F (32 °C), often reaching the mid-90s F (mid-30s C) or higher; summer nights are sultry and humid. Winters are cooler and more pleasant, with mean temperatures from December to March dipping to the low 70s F (low 20s C). Precipitation is confined to the winter months and averages only 3 inches (75 mm) per year, but this may vary from almost nothing to double that amount. On average, precipitation occurs only about 10 days a year. Sunshine is abundant year-round. The predominant wind is the damp, northwesterly *shamāl*; the *qaws*, a hot, dry south wind, is less frequent and brings sand, dust, and low humidity.

PLANT AND ANIMAL LIFE

Some 200 different species of desert plants grow in the bare, arid portions of the archipelago, while the irrigated and cultivated areas of the islands support fruit trees, fodder crops, and vegetables. The variety of animals is limited by the desert conditions. Gazelle and hares are not yet extinct, and lizards and jerboas (desert rodents) are common; the mongoose—probably imported from India—is found in the irrigated areas. Birdlife is sparse except in spring and autumn, when many varieties of migratory birds rest temporarily in Bahrain while traveling to and from higher temperate latitudes.

ETHNIC GROUPS

Roughly two-thirds of the population is Arab, and most are native-born Bahrainis, but some are Palestinians, Omanis, or Saudis. Foreign-born inhabitants, comprising more than one-third of the population, are mostly from Iran, India, Pakistan, Britain, and the United States. About three-fifths of the labour force is foreign.

LANGUAGES

Arabic is the official language of Bahrain. English is widely used, however, and is a compulsory second language at all schools. Persian is also common, although it is spoken mostly in the home. A number of other languages are spoken among expatriates in Bahrain, including Urdu, Hindi, and Tagalog.

RELIGION

The population is more than four-fifths Muslim and includes both the Sunni and Shīʿite sects, with the latter in the majority. The ruling family and many of the wealthier and more influential Bahrainis are Sunni, and this difference has been an underlying cause of local tension, particularly during and after the Iran-Iraq War (1980–88).

Manama

Manama (Arabic: Al-Manāmah) is the capital and largest city of the state and emirate of Bahrain. It lies at the northeast tip of Bahrain Island, in the Persian Gulf. About one-fifth of the emirate's population lives in the city. First mentioned in Islamic chronicles about 1345 CE, it was taken by the Portuguese (1521) and by the Persians (1602). It has been held, with brief interruptions, by the ruling Āl Khalīfah dynasty since 1783. Because Bahrain concluded a series of treaties (1861–1914) placing the country under increasing British protection, there was a British political agent stationed at Manama from 1900, subject to the political resident for the Persian Gulf, whose headquarters were long at Bushire, Iran. In 1946 the residency was moved to Manama, where it remained until the city became the capital of independent Bahrain in 1971.

Long an important commercial centre of the northern Persian Gulf, the traditional economy was based on pearling, fishing, boatbuilding, and import trade. Harbour facilities were poor; ocean vessels had to anchor in the open roadstead 2–4 miles (3–6 km) offshore. The discovery of petroleum on Bahrain (1932) revolutionized the city's economy and appearance, with the construction of many modern buildings. Manama developed as a trade, financial, and commercial centre; it is the seat of numerous banks. The headquarters of the Bahrain Petroleum Company (Bapco), however, are at ʿAwālī, in the centre of Bahrain Island. Manama was declared a free port in 1958, and the new deepwater facilities of Port Salmān, in the protected bay of al-Qulayʿah Inlet, southeast of the built-up area of the city, were opened in 1962. With storage and refrigeration facilities, and equipment for docking and repair of large oceangoing vessels, it is now one of the most important ports of the Persian Gulf. The island and town of Al-Muḥarraq lies just northeast; the two cities are linked by a causeway 1.5 miles (2.5 km) long.

Christians constitute about half of the remaining one-fifth of the population, with the rest consisting of Jews, Hindus, and Bahā'īs.

SETTLEMENT PATTERNS

The majority of the population now dwells in towns, but in the north and northwest of the main island, where irrigation has long been carried out using artesian water, there are numerous small villages and isolated dwellings where horticulture is the way of life. This area has an aspect of great fertility, which contrasts starkly with the bare desert appearance of much of the country. Villages consist, for the most part, of substantial flat-roofed houses built of stone or concrete. Some of the temporary settlements of fishermen and the poor are still constructed of *barasti* (branches of the date palm). There is little permanent settlement either in the southern half of Bahrain Island or on the smaller islands.

More than one-third of the population lives in the two principal cities, Manama and Al-Muḥarraq. Manama, with its Port Salmān, is the largest city and contains the main government offices, the business and financial district, many large hotels, Western-style shops, and a traditional Arab souk (market). It has a distinctly modern appearance as compared with Al-Muḥarraq, which is densely settled and has many narrow, winding streets. Other major settlements are 'Awālī, near the centre of Bahrain Island, built largely for expatriate employees of the Bahrain Petroleum Company B.S.C. (Bapco); Madīnat 'Īsā (Isa Town), a community established by the government in 1968; the sizable settlements of Al-Rifā' al-Shamālī (North Rifā'), Al-Rifā' al-Sharqī (East Rifā'), and Al-Rifā' al-Gharbī (West Rifā'); and Madīnat Ḥamad, completed in 1984.

DEMOGRAPHIC TRENDS

Although the population of Bahrain has been steadily growing, it has done so by narrowing margins since the turn of the 21st century. Life expectancy is high, with men living on average to about 72 and women to 77. The death rate is among the lowest in the world, and the major causes of death are diseases of the circulatory or respiratory system and cancer. Some one-fifth of the population is under the age of 15, and about one-half of the population is under age 30.

CHAPTER 2

The Bahraini Economy

Though it was the first emirate where oil was discovered (1932), Bahrain will most likely be the first to exhaust its reserves. Consequently, Bahrain has developed one of the most diversified economies in the Persian Gulf region. Bahrain's economic activity, like that of other Arab states in the Persian Gulf, has largely centred on the production of crude oil and natural gas and on refining petroleum products, making the country sensitive to fluctuations in the world oil market. Bahrain has built on its long tradition of shipping and commerce, however, and has been more successful than some other states in the gulf in developing manufacturing and commercial and financial services. The non-oil sector includes petrochemicals, ship repair, aluminum refining, and light manufacturing. The government-owned Aluminum Bahrain B.S.C. (Alba), one of the world's largest aluminum smelters, and Bapco have been profitable, but this has provided less incentive for privatization. Bahrain is one of the most important commercial and financial centres in the gulf, although it has faced growing competition from the United Arab Emirates.

Agriculture and Fishing

Less than 3 percent of Bahrain is arable, and agriculture contributes only a marginal proportion of the gross national product. The majority of Bahrain's food is imported, but agricultural production meets some local needs, including a large portion of vegetables and dairy products. Tomatoes, dates, bananas, citrus fruits, mangoes, pomegranates, and alfalfa (lucerne) are among the main crops. Cattle breeding and poultry farming are also encouraged by the government, while camels and horses

Deepwater oil-loading wharf off the island of Sitrah, Bahrain. FPG

are bred for racing. The increasingly polluted waters of the gulf, mainly caused by spillages from Kuwaiti oil installations during the Persian Gulf War, have killed off economically valuable marine life (notably shrimp) that were important to the fishing industry. Fisheries have remained largely unexploited in spite of some government attempts to privatize and modernize the industry.

RESOURCES AND POWER

Bahrain's oil production has always been small by Middle Eastern standards, and refining crude oil imported from Saudi Arabia has been of much greater importance since vast oil fields were discovered on the mainland; in 1998 Bapco began a major modernization project for its refinery. Bahrain's only oil field, Al-Baḥrayn (also known as Awali), is rapidly depleting. Several oil companies, however, have been granted exploration rights by the government. The country's offshore natural gas supplies are somewhat more substantial. Petroleum and natural gas resources and production are nationalized, but in the 1990s the government began encouraging foreign investment in the sector.

MANUFACTURING

The traditional industries of Bahrain were building dhows (lateen-rigged sailing vessels), fishing, pearling, and the manufacture of reed mats. These activities are now carried out on only a small scale.

Ship repair is handled at Port Salmān, near Manama, and at a large yard operated on Al-'Azl Island. Light industries include the production of building materials, furniture, soft drinks, plastics, and a wide range of consumer goods. The government has a significant financial stake in all these modern industries. In addition to the aluminum smelter operated by Alba, an aluminum rolling mill was opened in 1986 that manufactures such products as door and window frames.

FINANCE

The government has encouraged the growth of banking, insurance, and other financial services, and consequently Bahrain has become an important financial centre, notably of offshore banking. These activities have increasingly contributed to the country's balance of payments. Bahrain has also been able to benefit from its long tradition as a commercial centre. The country's central bank is the Bahrain Monetary Agency, which also issues the Bahraini dinar, the national currency. In addition to offshore banking units, there are local and foreign commercial banks, as well as investment banks. The Bahrain Stock Exchange opened in 1989.

TRADE

Bahrain's main import is the crude petroleum brought in by underwater pipeline from Saudi Arabia to be refined. Other major imports are machinery, vehicles, aluminum oxide, and food and live animals. The primary exports are refined petroleum products and aluminum goods. Saudi Arabia is the principal trading partner, and the United States and Japan are also important.

SERVICES

Services, including public administration, defense, and retail sales, employ a significant proportion of Bahrain's workforce and also account for about two-fifths of the gross domestic product. The service sector, particularly tourism, is a rapidly growing area of the economy.

Tourism is actively promoted by the government, and, with its balmy climate, scenic location, and sites of historic significance, the country is a growing tourist destination. Travelers from other, more conservative Persian Gulf countries—especially Saudi Arabia, which provides the largest number of visitors by far—are attracted to Bahrain's more liberal society. Visitors from outside the region come for the country's climate and to experience its unique cultural wealth.

LABOUR AND TAXATION

The majority of the workforce is men, with women constituting about one-fourth of the total. Women, however, are encouraged to work by the government, especially as a means of increasing indigenous employment. Beginning in the 1970s, non-Bahrainis have comprised a large portion of the country's workforce; by the end of the 20th century, two-thirds of those working were foreigners. There are no unions in Bahrain, which, although legal, are discouraged by the government. The standard workweek is Sunday through Thursday.

Bahrain has no individual income tax, and its only corporate tax is levied on oil, petroleum, and gas companies. Taxes account for only a small proportion of the country's revenue.

TRANSPORTATION AND TELECOMMUNICATIONS

Bahrain Island has an excellent system of paved roads, and its causeway connections to Al-Muḥarraq and Sitrah islands and to Saudi Arabia facilitate travel and tourism. There are no railroads, but the principal towns and villages are well served by bus and taxi services; a large proportion of residents also own motor vehicles. Bahrain International Airport on Al-Muḥarraq Island is one of the busiest airports in the Middle East and is served by most major international airlines. Manama is the headquarters of Gulf Air, once jointly owned by the governments of the gulf states but now under Bahraini ownership. Steamers run scheduled service from Bahrain to other gulf ports and to Pakistan and India.

Bahrain Telecommunications Company (Batelco), established in 1981, serves the country's telephone, wireless telephone, data communications, and Internet needs, either directly or through its subsidiaries. Through Batelco, Bahrain has promoted itself as a regional telecommunications centre, connecting the countries of the gulf region with the broader world. In 1998 Batelco opened an underwater fibre-optic cable network linking Bahrain, Kuwait, Qatar, and the United Arab Emirates.

CHAPTER 3

Bahraini Government and Society

Since the 18th century, the head of the Āl Khalīfah, the country's ruling family, has taken the title emir. A constitution promulgated in 2002 established Bahrain as a constitutional hereditary monarchy whose head of state is now titled king. Under the new constitution the executive is composed of a prime minister, who is head of government, and a Council of Ministers, all of whom are appointed by the king. The legislative branch consists of two houses: a 40-member Consultative Council that is also appointed by the king and a 40-member Chamber of Deputies that is elected by universal adult suffrage. The voting age is 20 years. Members of both deliberative bodies serve terms of four years. Women, in addition to voting, may stand for local and national elections.

An earlier constitution (1973) created a National Assembly composed of appointed members and others elected by popular vote, but after a period of labour unrest and political agitation the assembly was dissolved by the emir in 1975. Public representation thereupon reverted to the traditional Arab and Islamic system of a *majlis* (council), through which citizens and other residents presented petitions directly to the emir. In 1993 the emir created the Consultative Council, to which the first women were appointed in 2000.

JUSTICE

Bahrain's legal system is based on Sharīʿah (Islamic law) and English common law. The highest court in the country is the High Civil Appeals Court, and there are separate courts for members of Sunni and Shīʿite sects. When the royal family faced growing unrest in the 1990s from protesters, predominantly Shīʿite Muslims calling for a restoration of the constitution, a special court was established to prosecute dissenters.

POLITICAL PROCESS

In light of the political unrest of the 1990s, Ḥamad ibn ʿĪsā Āl Khalīfah, after succeeding his father to the throne in 1999, promised political reforms. In 2001 a national referendum approved a new document, the National Action

Bahrain's King Ḥamad ibn ʿĪsā Āl Khalīfa (left) *walks with Kuwait's crown prince, Sheikh Nawāf al-Aḥmad al-Ṣabāḥ, after the final session of the Gulf Cooperation Council (GCC) summit in Kuwait city on December 15, 2009. The GCC alliance is made up of Bahrain, Kuwait, Oman, Qatar, Saudi Arabia, and the United Arab Emirates.* Yasser Al-Zayyat/AFP/Getty Images

Charter (NAC), and the new constitution appeared the following year.

SECURITY

Participation in the military is voluntary, and males can enter service at age 15. The country maintains a large military and police force relative to its population, but it is one of the smallest in the region. In 1991, following the Persian Gulf War, Bahrain signed a defense cooperation agreement with the United States. Bahrain is the headquarters for the U.S. Navy's Fifth Fleet. The United Kingdom maintains a small military presence.

HEALTH AND WELFARE

Medical care is extensive and free, and there is provision for most forms of social security: pensions, sick pay, compensation for industrial injury, unemployment benefits, and maternity and family allowance payments. The government also sponsors public housing projects that are partially funded by its gulf neighbours.

HOUSING

Bahrain's constitution requires the government to help provide housing for any citizens unable to obtain adequate shelter through their own resources. Nearly three-fifths of all Bahrainis have benefited from government housing assistance in some way, and the government has likewise expended significant resources in recent decades to develop associated infrastructure. In 2001 the government inaugurated a new program to extend housing assistance to rural towns and villages.

EDUCATION

Bahrain's public education system, founded in 1932, is the oldest in the Arabian Peninsula. Public education is free for both boys and girls at the primary, intermediate, and secondary levels. Private and religious schools are available as well. The University of Bahrain, Arabian Gulf University, and the College of Health Sciences are institutions of higher learning. The vast majority of the population is literate, and Bahrain has one of the higher female literacy rates in the Persian Gulf.

CHAPTER 4

Bahraini Cultural Life

Bahrain's island location has made it unique among Persian Gulf states. With greater access to ocean travel and broader exposure to outside influences, Bahrain traditionally has been home to a more ethnically and religiously diverse and cosmopolitan population than have other, more insular gulf states. This openness is reflected in Bahrain's social customs, which—although still conservative—are much more moderate and relaxed than those of its neighbours, particularly conservative Saudi Arabia. Thus, although Bahrain is still at heart an Arab-Islamic country, it has been more accepting of modernization and Westernization than many of its neighbours.

DAILY LIFE AND SOCIAL CUSTOMS

The official holidays in Bahrain are generally the same as those observed in most Muslim countries. These include the two *ʿīd*s (festivals), ʿĪd al-Fiṭr and ʿĪd al-Aḍḥā, the Prophet Muhammad's birthday, and, more recently, the celebration of ʿĀshūrā among the country's Shīʿites.

Western-style clothing is common in Bahrain, though some men still wear the traditional *thawb* (full-length tunic) and the kaffiyeh (white head cloth), bound in place by a black, camel-hair cord known as an *ʿiqāl*—the latter often more ornate, particularly among the political elite. The dress rules for women are relaxed compared to the more conservative, regional standards, although women in rural areas, and those in conservative communities in cities, still wear the veil (*ḥijāb*) and a traditional long cloak known as an *ʿabāyah*.

Coffee is an important part of social life. Coffee shops are popular meeting places, and coffee is offered as a sign of hospitality. It is often flavoured with cardamom and saffron. Bahraini cuisine typically features fish, shrimp, meat, rice, and dates. *Machbous* is a popular traditional dish of fish or meat served with rice. Other typical food includes *muḥammar*, sweet brown rice with sugar or dates, and *shāwarmah*, spit-roasted lamb, beef, or chicken.

THE ARTS

Traditional handicraft industries receive state and popular support, and most villages practice specialized traditions; ʿĀlī, for example, is well known for its ceramics, while artists in Karbābād weave baskets from date-palm leaves. Throughout the country artisans engage in gold working, tinsmithing, and textile making and sell their wares at small shops or the Sūq al-Arabaʿā' ("Wednesday Market") in Manama. Shipyards at Manama and Al-Muḥarraq are sites of dhow building, a highly respected art form. The museum in Manama contains local artifacts dating from antiquity, such as ivory figurines, pottery, copper articles, and gold rings, many of which reflect various cultural influences from outside Bahrain. There is also a small but flourishing avant-garde art community.

Music is an important part of Bahraini life. There is a rich folk music culture, and *fidjeri*, songs once sung by pearl divers, are still heard. Since 1991 the country has held an annual music festival. Although the country's film industry is a relatively young one, moviegoing is a popular activity, and some of Bahrain's cinema theatres screen English-language films. In the early 21st century the government undertook a program to encourage the development of theatre.

ʿĪd al-Aḍḥā

ʿĪd al-Aḍḥā (Arabic: "Festival of Sacrifice"), also called ʿĪd al-Qurbān or al-ʿĪd al-Kabīr ("Major Festival"), is the second of two great Muslim festivals, the other being ʿĪd al-Fiṭr. ʿĪd al-Aḍḥā marks the culmination of the hajj (pilgrimage) rites at Minā, Saudi Arabia, near Mecca, but is celebrated by Muslims throughout the world. As with ʿĪd al-Fiṭr, it is distinguished by the performance of communal prayer (*ṣalāt*) at daybreak on its first day. It begins on the 10th of Dhu'l-Hijja, the last month of the Islamic calendar, and continues for an additional three days (though the Muslim use of a lunar calendar means that it may occur during any season of the year). During the festival, families that can afford to sacrifice a ritually acceptable animal (sheep, goat, camel, or cow) and then divide the flesh equally among themselves, the poor, and friends and neighbours. ʿĪd al-Aḍḥā is also a time for visiting with friends and family and for exchanging gifts. This festival commemorates the ransom with a ram of the biblical patriarch Ibrāhīm's (Abraham's) son Ismāʿīl (Ishmael)—rather than Isaac, in Judeo-Christian tradition.

Bahraini boys, wearing traditional outfits, count their pocket money for the Muslim holiday of Īd al-Aḍḥā in Manama. The three-day celebration marks the end of the annual Muslim pilgrimage to Mecca. Adam Jan/AFP/Getty Images

CULTURAL INSTITUTIONS

Bahrain has several museums, including the Bahrain National Museum and Beit al-Qur'ān, which houses a large collection of Qur'āns, some dating to the 7th century. There are also museums devoted to the history of petroleum production and to pearl diving as well as several art galleries. The Bahraini Ministry of Education maintains a network of public libraries, the oldest of which, in Manama, opened in 1946. The emirate also maintains one

Dhow

A dhow under construction in a boatyard on the coast of Bahrain. Tom Sheppard/Robert Harding Picture Library

A dhow is a one- or two-masted Arab sailing vessel, usually with lateen rigging (slanting, triangular sails), common in the Red Sea and the Indian Ocean. On the larger types, called baggalas and booms, the mainsail is considerably bigger than the mizzensail. Bows are sharp, with a forward and upward thrust, and the sterns of the larger dhows may be windowed and decorated.

of the principal wildlife conservation areas in the Persian Gulf region, Al-Areen Park, which harbours such indigenous mammals as the oryx and gazelle and is visited by many waterfowl species.

SPORTS AND RECREATION

Football (soccer) is the most popular modern sport, while horse racing remains a national pastime. More than 20 types of Arabian horses are bred on the islands, and races are held weekly on Bahrain Island's large racecourse, which seats some 10,000 spectators. Traditional sports such as falconry and gazelle and hare hunting are still practiced by wealthier Bahrainis, and camel racing is a popular public entertainment. The country first competed in the Olympics at the 1984 Summer Games.

MEDIA AND PUBLISHING

Several weekly and daily papers are published in Arabic; others appear in English. Most of the press is privately owned and is not subject to censorship as long as it refrains from criticizing the ruling family. The state television and radio stations broadcast most programs in Arabic, although there are channels in English.

CHAPTER 5

Bahrain: Past and Present

Bahrain has been inhabited since prehistoric times, and several thousand burial mounds in the northern part of the main island probably date from the Sumerian period of the 3rd millennium BCE. It was the seat of ancient Dilmun (Telmun), a prosperous trading centre linking Sumeria with the Indus Valley about 2000 BCE. The archipelago was mentioned by Persian, Greek, and Roman geographers and historians. It has been Arab and Muslim since the Muslim conquest of the 7th century CE, though it was ruled by the Portuguese from 1521 to 1602 and by the Persians from 1602 to 1783. Since 1783 it has been ruled by sheikhs of the Khalīfah family (Āl Khalīfah), which originated in the Al-Hasa (Al-Ḥasā) province of Arabia.

The British Protectorate

Several times during the 19th century, the British intervened to suppress war and piracy and to prevent the establishment of Egyptian, Persian, German, or Russian spheres of influence. The first Bahraini-British treaty was signed in 1820, although the country's British-protected status dates from 1861, with the completion of a treaty by which the sheikh agreed to refrain from "the prosecution of war, piracy, or slavery." Thus, Britain assumed responsibility for the defense of Bahrain and for the conduct of its relations with other major powers. In 1947 this protection briefly became the responsibility of the government of British India, which had both commercial and strategic interests in the Persian Gulf, but it reverted to Britain following India's independence. Until 1970 the government

Dilmun

Dilmun is the Sumerian name of an ancient independent kingdom that flourished *c.* 2000 BCE, centred on Bahrain Island in the Persian Gulf. Dilmun is mentioned as a commercial centre in Sumerian economic texts of the late 4th millennium BCE, when it was a transshipment point for goods between Sumer and the Indus Valley. Copper and a variety of other goods, including stone beads, precious stones, pearls, dates, and vegetables, were shipped to Sumer and Babylonia in return for agricultural products.

Bārbār, the remains of an ancient temple (largely built of limestone) situated on Bahrain Island, and many thousands of burial mounds attest to the island's prominence. Qala'at (fort) al-Baḥrain, a large low tell covering about 45 acres (18 hectares) on the northern coast of the island, is the largest site and was designated a UNESCO World Heritage site in 2005. It consists of a city dating from about 2800 BCE that had seven major building phases including, in its second phase (2300–1800 BCE), city walls; other artifacts found dating to this phase are chert weights of the Indus Valley type, distinctive round steatite stamp seals, and quantities of copper. Related archaeological sites have been found on the northern coast of the Arabian Peninsula and on other offshore islands in the Persian Gulf.

of Iran periodically advanced claims to sovereignty over Bahrain, but these were repudiated.

Britain's decision to withdraw all of its forces from the gulf in 1968 led Sheikh 'Isā ibn Sulmān Āl Khalīfah to proclaim Bahrain's independence in August 1971. A treaty of friendship was signed with the United Kingdom, terminating Bahrain's status as a British protectorate, and Sheikh 'Īsā was designated the emir. Bahrain then became a member of the United Nations and the Arab League.

DOMESTIC AND FOREIGN RELATIONS SINCE INDEPENDENCE

After independence, tensions mounted between the predominantly Shīʿite population and Sunni leadership—especially following the 1979 revolution in Iran. The political unrest was fueled by economic and social grievances related to the fall in oil prices and production, cutbacks in public spending, and continued discrimination against the majority Shīʿite population.

In 1981 Bahrain joined with five other Arab gulf states in forming the Gulf Cooperation Council (GCC), which has led to freer trading and closer economic and defense ties. During the Persian Gulf War (1990–91), Bahrain made its port and airfields available to the U.S. coalition forces that drove Iraqi forces out of Kuwait. Although more moderate than Saudi Arabia, Bahrain has generally followed that country's lead in most foreign policy decisions. The construction of the causeway linking Bahrain with Saudi Arabia has strengthened bilateral relations and regional defense and has helped both countries economically and politically. Bahrain has maintained relatively good relations with the United States and has continued to house the U.S. Navy's Fifth Fleet. Iran's ties to the country's Shīʿite community, its territorial claims to the island, and its displeasure with the American presence in Bahrain have helped to strain relations between it and Bahrain. Resolution in 2001 of the dispute between Bahrain and Qatar over the Ḥawār Islands improved their already warming relations.

Sheikh Ḥamad ibn ʿIsā Āl Khalīfah, who assumed power on the death of his father in March 1999, released a number of imprisoned Shīʿite dissidents and other individuals later that year in a bid to ease tensions. These changes led in 2001 to a referendum—overwhelmingly supported by Bahrainis—that ratified the National Action Charter. The charter was followed in 2002 with the promulgation of a new constitution that established a constitutional monarchy in Bahrain, called for equality between Sunnis and Shīʿites, and guaranteed civil and property rights to all citizens.

The country's first municipal and parliamentary elections in decades were held in May and October 2002, respectively. The municipal election marked the first time that female candidates were able to run for public office. In the parliamentary election in October, no women were elected to the lower house of the bicameral parliament, although some did receive appointment to the upper house. In the 2006 elections, Bahrain elected a woman to parliament for the first time. Even as Bahraini political life

Economic issues still cause tensions in Bahrain. Here, Bahrainis waving banners march in the streets of Manama on January 8, 2010, as they protest a government decision to lift subsidies on fuel and gas. Adam Jan/AFP/ Getty Images

becomes increasingly inclusive, however, the country has not reached complete democratization.

Economically, high rates of unemployment—among the highest in the gulf region, and a special concern among the country's youth—are a particularly significant concern. In 2009 sponsorship of expatriate workers was reduced, an initiative meant to address unemployment among native Bahrainis.

In 2008 King Ḥamad initiated a new economic diversification plan meant to reduce reliance on petroleum and boost Bahrainis' disposable income.

With its business and leisure tourism industry, aluminum processing facilities, shipbuilding and ship repair industry, and the promotion of Bahrain as a centre of Islamic banking, at the end of the first decade of the 21st century, Bahrain appeared well placed to thrive in a post-petroleum era.

CHAPTER 6

Kuwait: The Land and Its People

Kuwait is slightly larger in area than the U.S. state of Hawaii and is bounded to the west and north by Iraq, to the east by the Persian Gulf, and to the south by Saudi Arabia.

Kuwait is largely a desert, except for Al-Jahrā' oasis, at the western end of Kuwait Bay, and a few fertile patches in the southeastern and coastal areas. Kuwaiti territory includes nine offshore islands, the largest of which are the uninhabited Būbiyān and Al-Warbah. The island of Faylakah, which is located near the entrance of Kuwait Bay, has been populated since prehistoric times.

A territory of 2,200 square miles (5,700 square km) along the gulf was shared by Kuwait and Saudi Arabia as a neutral zone until a political boundary was agreed on in 1969. Each of the two countries now administers half of the territory (called the Neutral, or Partitioned, Zone), but they continue to share equally the revenues from oil production in the entire area. Although the boundary with Saudi Arabia is defined, the border with Iraq remains in dispute.

The population of Kuwait is chiefly Arab. However, because of the large proportion of guest workers—who constitute some two-thirds of the entire population—Kuwaitis are a minority in their own country. Historically, there were several important class divisions in Kuwait. These divisions emerged during the period when the country was a trade entrepôt and were largely economic; thus, as the state became Kuwait's primary employer after oil was discovered in the 1930s and these reserves were commercially developed in subsequent decades, this class structure became less pronounced. The one historically important class that remains politically important is the

The Kuwait Towers, containing two water reservoirs and a restaurant with a revolving viewing platform, Kuwait city, Kuwait. Burnett H. Moody/ Bruce Coleman Inc.

old merchant oligarchy, the Banū (Banī) ʿUtūb—of which the ruling family is a member.

RELIEF

The relief of Kuwait is generally flat or gently undulating, broken only by occasional low hills and shallow depressions. The elevations range from sea level in the east to 951 feet (290 metres) above sea level at Al-Shiqāyā peak, in the western corner of the country. The Al-Zawr Escarpment, one of the main topographic features, borders the northwestern shore of Kuwait Bay and rises to a maximum elevation of 475 feet (145 metres). Elsewhere in coastal areas, large patches of salty marshland have developed. Throughout the northern, western, and central sections of Kuwait, there are desert basins, which fill with water after winter rains; historically these basins formed important watering places, refuges for the camel herds of the Bedouin.

DRAINAGE

Kuwait has no permanent surface water, either in the form of standing bodies such as lakes or in the form of flows such

Faylakah

Faylakah is an island of Kuwait lying in the Persian Gulf near the entrance to Kuwait Bay; it has an area of 15 square miles (39 square km). Inhabited since prehistoric times, it is important archaeologically, remains of human habitation from as early as 2500 BCE having been found there. A museum has been built near the ruins of a Greek temple. Most of the people live in the village of Al-Zawr, on the island's northwestern tip. Fishing and labouring in the archaeological diggings are the principal occupations, but the island has also become a resort.

as perennial rivers. Intermittent water courses (wadis) are localized and generally terminate in interior desert basins. Little precipitation is absorbed beyond the surface level, with most being lost to evaporation.

SOILS

True soils scarcely exist naturally in Kuwait. Those that exist are of little agricultural productivity and are marked by an extremely low amount of organic matter. Eolian soils and other sedimentary deposits are common, and a high degree of salinity is found, particularly in basins and other locations where residual water pools. One of the environmental consequences of the Persian Gulf War was the widespread destruction of the desert's rigid surface layer, which held underlying sand deposits in place; this has led to an increase in wind-borne sand and the

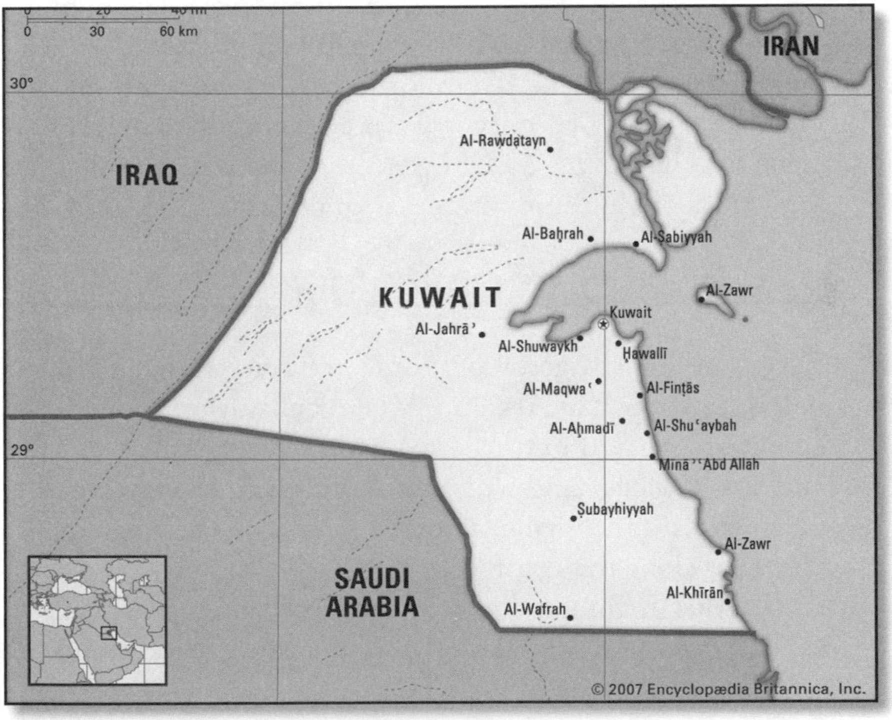

creation of larger and more numerous sand dunes in the country.

CLIMATE

The climate is desert, tempered somewhat in the coastal regions by the warm waters of the gulf. If there is enough precipitation, the desert turns green from mid-March to the end of April. But during the dry season, between April and September, the heat is severe—daytime temperatures ordinarily reach into the 110s F (mid-40s C) and on occasion approach 130 °F (54 °C). The winter is more agreeable (frost can even occasionally occur in the interior, though never on the seacoast). Annual precipitation levels average only from 1 to 7 inches (25 to 180 mm), chiefly between October and April, though cloudbursts can bring more than 2 inches (50 mm) of precipitation in a single day.

The frequent winds from the northwest are cool in winter and spring and hot in summer. Southeasterly winds, usually hot and damp, spring up between July and October; hot and dry south winds prevail in spring and early summer. The *shamāl*, a northwesterly wind common during June and July, causes dramatic sandstorms.

PLANT AND ANIMAL LIFE

Except in the new green belt of Kuwait city and in a few desert oases such as Al-Jahrāʾ, where cultivation and irrigation are carried out, the vegetation consists of scrub and low bushes (and ephemeral grass in the spring). Halophytes (salt-loving plants) grow on the marshy stretches along the coast.

The harsh climate limits mammals to the occasional gazelle, fox, or civet. Among lizards are the rare and venomous sand viper (*Cerastes vipera*) and the monitor and vegetarian dab lizards (*Uromastix spinipes*).

ETHNIC GROUPS

In spite of a government policy to reduce the number of foreign workers following the Iraqi invasion in 1990, Kuwaitis remain a minority in their own country. Nearly two-thirds of the population are expatriate workers, chiefly from South and Southeast Asia as well as from other Arab states. These nonnationals do not enjoy citizenship rights, economic or political, which are reserved for Kuwaiti citizens—defined as those able to prove Kuwaiti ancestry prior to 1920. Naturalization is strictly limited. Arabs—either Bedouin, sedentary, or descendants of immigrants from elsewhere in the region—constitute the largest ethnic group, and a small number of ethnic Persians have resided in the country for centuries.

LANGUAGES

The native and official language is Arabic, fluency in which is a requirement for naturalization. Kuwaitis speak a dialect of Gulf Arabic, and Modern Standard Arabic is taught in schools. English is the second language taught in public schools. Hindi, Urdu, Persian (Farsi), and other languages also are widely spoken among the foreign population.

RELIGION

Kuwaiti citizens are almost entirely Muslim, and a law passed in 1981 limits citizenship to Muslims. The majority are Sunni, but about one-sixth are Shīʿite. Both the Iranian revolution of 1979 and the Kuwaiti government's subsequent discrimination against Shīʿites fostered a heightened sense of community among the country's Shīʿite population in the 1980s and '90s, and this led to political tension between the two groups.

SETTLEMENT PATTERNS

The old town of Kuwait, although located in a harsh desert climate, opened onto an excellent sheltered harbour. Kuwait developed in the 18th and 19th centuries as a trading city, relying on the pearl banks of the gulf as well as on long-distance sea and caravan traffic. The old city—facing the sea and bounded landward from 1918 to 1954 by a mud wall, the gates of which led out into the desert—was compact, only 5 square miles (13 square km) in area; its typical dwelling was a courtyard house. After the discovery of oil in the 1930s and the petroleum industry's rapid expansion after World War II, Kuwait city underwent a transformation. The ensuing urban explosion led to the destruction of the semicircular city wall (its gates were preserved as a reminder of the early years), and city planners formally laid out new suburbs. The government invested large portions of oil revenues in infrastructure and urban development, creating in the process a modern metropolis.

Kuwaitis are now scattered at a relatively low density throughout the urban area and surrounding suburbs. Non-Kuwaitis, largely excluded from the restricted suburbs, live at higher densities in the old city and in the suburbs of Ḥawallī and Al-Sālimiyyah, mostly in apartments.

DEMOGRAPHIC TRENDS

Until the Iraqi invasion, Palestinians, some of them third-generation residents of Kuwait, were the largest single expatriate group, numbering perhaps 400,000. Popular

Kuwait City

ʿAbd Allāh al-Mubarraq al-Ṣabāḥ Mosque in the city of Kuwait. Tor Eigeland/Black Star

Kuwait (Arabic: Al-Kuwayt) is the national capital of Kuwait. The city lies on the southern shore of Kuwait Bay of the Persian Gulf. Its name is a diminutive of the Arabic *kūt* ("fort").

Kuwait city was founded at the beginning of the 18th century by a group of families who migrated to the coast from the interior of the Arabian Peninsula. The old mud-walled city, only about 5 square miles (13 square km) in area, made its livelihood by fishing, pearling, and trading with the Indian subcontinent and eastern Africa. It was long the only populated place of consequence in the country.

With the development of Kuwait's petroleum industry after World War II, Kuwait city and the surrounding area, including the residential suburb of Ḥawallī, began to grow rapidly. The mud wall was torn down in 1957, and only three gates remain. The city rapidly became a flourishing administrative, commercial, and financial centre, with modern hotel and high-rise office buildings; its banking facilities were among the largest in the Middle East. Kuwait city has many luxurious residences, as well as a number of parks and gardens; tree-lined avenues carry heavy automobile traffic. Kuwait University opened in 1966; the city's historical museum exhibits artifacts from Faylakah island.

When Iraq invaded and occupied Kuwait (August 1990 to February 1991) during the Persian Gulf War, Iraqi forces systematically stripped Kuwait city of its food supplies, consumer goods, equipment, and other movable assets, and many of the city's inhabitants fled the country. Kuwait city suffered considerable damage to buildings and infrastructure, but after the war Kuwaitis were able to return to their capital and much of the city was rebuilt.

Palestinian support for Iraq during the war and persistent Palestinian demands for political inclusion led the Kuwaiti government to deport most of them following the restoration of authority, and by early 1992 their number had fallen to 50,000. They have been largely replaced by Egyptians, Syrians, Iranians, and South Asians.

Life expectancy in Kuwait is high, with men living to about 76 years and women to 79 years. Although Kuwait's birth rate is only slightly higher than the world average, its death rate—one of the world's lowest—has led to a high rate of natural increase. The leading cause of death is circulatory disease. The country is young, with one-half of the population under the age of 30.

CHAPTER 7

The Kuwaiti Economy

Virtually all of Kuwait's wealth is derived directly or indirectly, by way of overseas investments, from petroleum extraction and processing. The most dramatic element of Kuwait's economic development has been the steady and rapid expansion of its oil industry since the 1970s. By the mid-1980s Kuwait was refining four-fifths of its oil domestically and marketing some 250,000 barrels a day in its own European retail outlets under the name "Q8." This oil income and the investment income it generated—the latter surpassed direct sales of oil revenues by the 1980s—gave Kuwait one of the highest per capita incomes in the world. Although both the Iraqi invasion (which nearly exhausted Kuwait's overseas investment revenues) and the increasing volatility of the global oil market in the 1980s reduced this income substantially, income levels rebounded when oil prices rose dramatically in the early 21st century. Other sectors of Kuwait's economy are weak by comparison; agriculture, manufacturing, and trade each constitute only a small proportion of the country's gross domestic product (GDP).

Agriculture and Fishing

The possibilities of agricultural development are severely limited. Only a small amount of the land is arable, and, because of scarcity of water, soil deficiencies, and lack of workers trained in agricultural skills, only a portion of that land area is under actual cultivation. Agriculture's contribution, therefore, is insignificant to the output of the economy.

Fish are plentiful in the Persian Gulf, and fishing in Kuwait was a leading industry before the discovery of oil.

The United Fisheries of Kuwait continues the tradition today. Shrimp was one of the few commodities besides oil that Kuwait continued to export after World War II. Shrimp production was devastated by the environmental havoc wreaked in the gulf by the Persian Gulf War.

RESOURCES AND POWER

Kuwait has nearly one-tenth of the world's proven oil reserves. Kuwait's proven recoverable reserves are thought to be enough to sustain current production levels for some 150 years, and, though the oil industry sustained severe damage during the Iraqi invasion, most of that was repaired by the mid-1990s. Kuwait also has considerable natural gas reserves, almost all in the form of associated gas—i.e., gas that is produced together with crude oil. Significant quantities of other minerals are not known. Naturally occurring fresh water is scarce; until desalination plants were built after World War II, water had to be imported.

The generation of electricity also has increased significantly as population and industry have grown. Production is concentrated in several large natural gas-fired power stations, including one at Al-Shuwaykh and another at Al-Shuʿaybah.

Oil

In 1934 the Kuwait Oil Company (KOC), the ownership of which was divided equally between what were then the British Petroleum Company and the Gulf Oil Corporation (of the United States), obtained a concession covering the whole territory except the Neutral Zone. Oil was struck in 1938, but World War II deferred development until 1946. Thereafter, progress was spectacular. In

Oil rig in the Persian Gulf off Kuwait. © Piergiorgio Sclarandis/Black Star

1953 the American Independent Oil Company and the Getty Oil Company, which jointly held concessions for the Neutral Zone, struck oil in commercial quantities, and in 1955 oil was discovered in northern Kuwait. By 1976 Kuwait had achieved complete control of the KOC, with the former owners retaining the right to purchase at a discount. The government also achieved full ownership of the Kuwait National Petroleum Company (KNPC), which it had formed in 1960 with private Kuwaiti investors. The KNPC, designed to serve as an integrated oil company, controlled the supply and distribution of petroleum products within the country and began marketing operations abroad. In 1980 the government founded the Kuwait Petroleum Corporation as an umbrella organization overseeing the KOC and the KNPC as well as the Kuwait Oil Tanker Company, the Petrochemicals

Industries Company, and the Kuwait Foreign Petroleum Exploration Company.

The relatively low cost of oil production in Kuwait stems from certain unique advantages. Most important, there are a number of highly productive wells, the output of which can be varied at short notice, which thus eliminates the need for large numbers of storage tanks. Most of the storage tanks themselves are placed on a ridge set back a few miles from the seacoast at a height of some 300 feet (90 metres); this enables loading operations to be carried out by gravity rather than by pumps. There are also extensive refineries and bunkers for tankers. While retreating from Kuwait at the end of the Persian Gulf War, Iraqi forces set fire to more than 700 of the country's 950 wells. By the fall of 1991, the fires, which had consumed about six million barrels of oil per day, had been extinguished, and production soon returned to preinvasion levels.

Natural Gas

Massive volumes of natural gas are produced in association with crude oil. Although natural gas has great potential as a source of foreign exchange, it principally has been used for reinjection in oil fields to maintain pressure, generating electricity (notably for water distillation), and producing (as raw material) petrochemicals and fertilizers, some of which Kuwait exports in small quantities.

Water

For fresh water in earlier days, people depended on a few artesian wells and on rainwater collected from the roofs of houses or from cisterns at ground level. Dhows piloted by Kuwaiti seamen also brought fresh water from the Shatt al-Arab near Al-Başrah, Iraq. With the rapid growth of population, however, the government of Kuwait built desalination plants at Kuwait city, Al-Shu'aybah, and several other locations. Important sources of fresh water have been discovered at Al-Rawḍatayn and Al-Shiqāyā, but desalination still provides the great bulk of Kuwait's daily consumption of potable water.

MANUFACTURING

Manufacturing, which contributes only minimally to Kuwait's GDP, consists almost entirely of refined petroleum products, petrochemicals, and fertilizers. Other, less-important manufactured products include clothing and apparel, fabricated metal products, industrial chemicals, and nonelectrical machinery.

FINANCE

The Central Bank of Kuwait issues the national currency, the Kuwaiti dinar, and is the country's main banking regulatory body. In addition to its central bank, Kuwait has specialized banks operating in the areas of savings and credit, industrial loans, and real estate. There are also commercial banks. No foreign banks may operate in Kuwait, with the exception of the Bank of Bahrain and Kuwait, based in Bahrain and owned equally by the two states. An Islamic bank—one bound by stringent religious laws governing financial transactions—has also been established. Before independence an officially sanctioned stock exchange operated, growing to become one of the largest in the world. The fall of the unofficial but wildly popular stock market, the Sūq al-Manākh, in 1982 sent the local economy into a mild recession. A resulting debt-settlement program supervised by the government was not completed until the early 21st century.

TRADE

Petroleum and petroleum-derived products account for all but a very minor portion of Kuwait's exports. Kuwait's imports consist largely of machinery and transport equipment, manufactured goods, and food. The country's primary trading partners include Japan, the United States, and China.

SERVICES

Kuwait has invested only marginally in local industry. As a result, nearly all employed Kuwaitis work for the state, largely in education (only a small fraction of these are in the oil industry). Almost one-third of the government's revenues are spent on salaries. Tourism plays only a small role in the country's economy. The Iraqi invasion further limited its importance, and the sector was slow to recover. The vast majority of tourists are from Saudi Arabia.

LABOUR AND TAXATION

In both the public and private sectors, Kuwait remains heavily dependent on foreign labour, in spite of repeated reforms aimed at reducing this dependency. In the early 21st century, only about one-sixth of the country's workforce were Kuwaiti nationals. Trade unions are allowed, but numerous restrictions limit their establishment. Less than one-tenth of the country's workforce belongs to a union.

Kuwait has no individual income tax. Much of the government's revenue comes from oil as well as from taxes on foreign corporations and on the foreign interests of Kuwaiti companies.

TRANSPORTATION AND TELECOMMUNICATIONS

Although there are no railways in the country, Kuwait has a modern road system linking it with its neighbours, as well as a large international airport, Kuwait International Airport, which is located just south of the capital. Kuwait Airways Corporation, a state-owned enterprise, serves a number of international routes. The country's port facilities and its fleet of oil tankers and general cargo ships have been expanded.

Regular telephone service was established in Kuwait only in the 1950s; since that time the country has made significant progress in telephone, cable, wireless communication, and Internet service. The country's communication infrastructure was badly damaged during the Iraqi invasion, but the damage has largely been repaired, and the Kuwaiti government—through its Ministry of Communications—has further developed Kuwait's communication grid by means of contracts with international telecommunications firms.

CHAPTER 8

Kuwaiti Government and Society

Kuwait is a constitutional monarchy with one legislative body. Since gaining independence from Britain in 1961, Kuwait has been governed by an emir from the Ṣabāḥ family. The emir rules through a Council of Ministers—consisting largely of members of his own family—that he himself appoints. Legislative power rests in the National Assembly (Majlis al-Ummah), whose 50 members are elected to four-year terms. This parliament, however, was suspended a number of times, including in 1976, in 1985, and again in 1999.

JUSTICE

Kuwait's legal system has several sources. Personal and civil law (roughly, family law and probate law) are based largely on Sharīʿah (Islamic law). Commercial and criminal law, while also influenced by Sharīʿah, borrows heavily from both European civil and common law as well as from the legal codes of the Ottoman Empire and from those of other Arab states, which are themselves heavily influenced by European law. There are several lower courts and a system of appeals courts. The emir sometimes acts as the final court of appeal.

POLITICAL PROCESS

In lieu of political parties, which are prohibited in Kuwait, several quasi-political organizations have representatives in the parliament. Voting is limited to natural-born Kuwaiti men who are at least 21 years old; servicemen and police are barred from voting. Under these qualifications, approximately one-tenth of the population forms the electorate. Beginning in the 1990s, attempts to extend suffrage to women increased. In 1999 the emir announced that he would allow women to vote in future elections; the franchise was officially granted in 2005, and in 2009 women were elected to parliament for the first time.

SECURITY

Kuwait's military expenditure per capita is among the highest in the world. Such spending is largely a result of the hostile relationship with Iraq; after the Persian Gulf War, Kuwait undertook significant measures to modernize and increase its armed forces. U.S. troops have been stationed there since the early 1990s, and Kuwait also has defense agreements with other countries, including Russia, the United Kingdom, and France. Kuwaiti males are required to serve two years in the armed forces, although university students may receive exemptions for one year of that service.

Ṣabāḥ Dynasty

The Ṣabāḥ dynasty (or Āl Ṣabāḥ, "Ṣabāḥ family") has been the ruling family of Kuwait since 1756. In that year the Banū 'Utūb, a group of families of the 'Anizah tribe living in what is now Kuwait, appointed a member of the Ṣabāḥ family, Ṣabāḥ ibn Jābir (ruled *c.* 1752–64), to be their ruler. The dynasty frequently depended politically or militarily on outsiders but maintained its autonomy. Its dependence on the Ottoman Empire in the late 19th century was subsequently a cause for Iraq to claim hegemony over Kuwait. It later enjoyed the patronage of the United Kingdom and, more recently, the support of the U.S. In spite of the existence of deliberative institutions in modern Kuwait, the dynasty retains absolute power.

HEALTH AND WELFARE

Kuwait has a comprehensive scheme of social welfare. The needy receive financial assistance; loans are provided to the handicapped to start businesses; the disabled can get treatment and training; and education is available for adult illiterates. The Ministry of Social Affairs offers a program that provides adequate, affordable housing, fully equipped with modern facilities, for citizens with limited incomes. Kuwait also has a comprehensive and highly developed subsidized national health-care system. In 1976 the government established Kuwait's Reserve Fund for Future Generations, and it has set aside 10 percent of the state's revenues annually for it. The government found it necessary, however, to tap into that fund during the Iraqi occupation.

HOUSING

Housing in Kuwait is heavily subsidized by the government, and—since the government has invested large amounts of money in development since the oil boom—housing standards are generally high. Traditional housing (mud-walled structures one to two stories tall) has largely given way to modern-style homes and apartment complexes in most parts of the country.

EDUCATION

More than four-fifths of the population is literate. General education in Kuwait is compulsory for native Kuwaitis between the ages of 6 and 14. It is entirely free and also includes school meals, books, uniforms, transportation, and medical attention. Non-Kuwaiti students typically

Students gather on campus at Kuwait University after voting in student union elections on October 22, 2009. Yasser Al-Zayyat/AFP/Getty Images

attend private schools. Kuwait University was founded in 1964. The vast majority of its students are Kuwaitis, and about three-fifths are women. In 2001 the university began segregating by gender, a move that was called for by the National Assembly. Other institutions of higher learning include the College of Technological Studies. The American University of Kuwait was established in 2004. Several thousand students attend colleges and universities overseas, principally in the United States, Britain, and Egypt, usually on state scholarships.

CHAPTER 9

Kuwaiti Cultural Life

Although Kuwait embraces many facets of Western culture, Arab-Islamic heritage permeates daily life, and the country remains culturally conservative. As in much of the Middle East, the rise of Islamic fundamentalism in the 1970s and ’80s was reflected in a general return to traditional customs, as seen in the public dress of women, who began wearing the *ḥijāb*, or veil, far more than in the past. The right of women to drive automobiles and to work outside the home is generally accepted and has not been a matter of public debate, yet the question of granting women the right to vote has divided Islamists, some of whom seek to enforce even more conservative Islamic standards, such as those found in neighbouring Saudi Arabia.

Daily Life and Social Customs

At the heart of traditional Kuwaiti culture is the institution of the *diwāniyyah*, a regular gathering of men—usually in a tent or a separate room of the main house—which serves as a time to gather, enjoy refreshments, talk, or play games. Kuwaitis observe all major Islamic holidays, including Ramadan and the two *ʿīds* (festivals), ʿĪd al-Fiṭr and ʿĪd al-Aḍḥā. The country’s Independence Day and Liberation Day (from the Iraqi occupation of 1990–91) are important secular holidays.

Fūl, falafel, and hummus are the cornerstones of Kuwaiti cuisine, though Western fast-food restaurants abound in Kuwait city. *Fūl* is a paste based on fava beans, with garlic and lemon added. Falafel, a fried food made from chickpeas and spices, is often served in unleavened

A Kuwaiti vendor sells dates at a market during the second day of the Muslim holy month of Ramadan in Kuwait city on September 2, 2008. Yasser Al-Zayyat/AFP/Getty Images

bread (*khubz*) with vegetables. Chickpeas are also used to make hummus, a dip for vegetables and bread. The traditional Kuwaiti meal consists of spiced rice topped with meat or fish or shellfish taken from the Persian Gulf.

THE ARTS

Kuwaiti folk arts remain important, and Bedouin crafts are the most prominent. Though few Bedouins now inhabit Kuwait, their art traditions, especially weaving, have been maintained. The intricately woven fabrics are made on a *sadu*, a Bedouin loom, and are common sights in souks (bazaars). Sadu House, a museum for Bedouin crafts, offers classes on weaving. Also popular are traditional dances, including the *ʿarḍah*, which features swords and poetry singing. The government supports the preservation of folk arts and funds numerous organizations, as well as several troupes that perform across the country.

CULTURAL INSTITUTIONS

Kuwait has numerous museums, but the Iraqi invasion had a disastrous effect on many institutions. Many artworks were stolen by the Iraqis, and some buildings were severely damaged. The National Museum of Kuwait, which once housed a comprehensive collection of Islamic art, was looted and set ablaze; only a small portion of the building has been renovated and reopened to the public. The loss has increased the importance of the Tareq Rajab Museum, a private collection that features paintings, pottery, metalwork, jewelry, and musical instruments, among other items.

SPORTS AND RECREATION

Kuwait's sports culture, like that of other gulf states, combines the traditional sports of nomadic Arabian society with contemporary sports of Western origin. Traditional sports of enduring popularity include camel and horse racing; Arabian horses are held to be among the finest in the world. Falconry is enjoyed primarily by the wealthy, although the overhunting of game and, after 1990, the presence of unexploded land mines in the desert have reduced its practice. Kuwaitis have competed at the national and international levels in the country's two most widely played sports, football (soccer) and golf. Oil revenues have enabled the government to support sports generously, and the country boasts a number of stadiums capable of hosting international competitions. The country's first trip to the Olympics came with its participation in the 1968 Summer Games.

MEDIA AND PUBLISHING

The Ministry of Information runs the government press and the radio and television broadcasting stations. Much of the print media receives financial support from the government. Although the constitution guarantees freedom of the press, this right has often been suspended. In 1992 print restrictions were relaxed on the condition that the media sources monitor themselves. The Kuwaiti media today is generally outspoken and is free by regional standards; direct criticism of the emir, however, as well as statements considered insulting to religion, are still prohibited.

CHAPTER 10

Kuwait: Past and Present

The origin of the city of Kuwait—and of the State of Kuwait—is usually placed at about the beginning of the 18th century, when the Banū (Banī) 'Utūb, a group of families of the 'Anizah tribe in the interior of the Arabian Peninsula, migrated to the area that is now Kuwait. The foundation of the autonomous sheikhdom of Kuwait dates from 1756, when the settlers decided to appoint a sheikh from the Ṣabāḥ family (Āl Ṣabāḥ).

KUWAIT FROM THE 19TH CENTURY TO INDEPENDENCE

During the 19th century, Kuwait developed as a thriving, independent trading community. Toward the end of the century, one ruler, 'Abd Allāh II (ruled 1866–92), began to move Kuwait closer to the Ottoman Empire, although he never placed his country under Ottoman rule. This trend was reversed with the accession of Mubārak the Great, who came to power by assassinating his brother 'Abd Allāh—an act of uncustomary political violence in Kuwait. Ottoman threats to annex Kuwait prompted Mubārak to cultivate a close relationship with Britain. An 1899 treaty basically granted Britain control of Kuwait's foreign affairs. Following the outbreak of World War I (1914–18), Kuwait became a British protectorate.

At the 1922 Conference of Al-'Uqayr, Britain negotiated the Kuwait-Saudi border, with substantial territorial loss to Kuwait. A memorandum in 1923 set out the border with Iraq on the basis of an unratified 1913 convention.

The first Iraqi claim to Kuwait surfaced in 1938—the year oil was discovered in the emirate. Although neither Iraq nor the Ottoman Empire had ever actually ruled

Kuwait, Iraq asserted a vague historical title. That year it also offered some rhetorical support to a merchant uprising against the emir. Following the failure of the uprising, called the Majlis Movement, Iraq continued to put forth a claim to at least part of Kuwait, notably the strategic islands of Būbiyān and Al-Warbah.

On June 19, 1961, Britain recognized Kuwait's independence. Six days later, however, Iraq renewed its claim, which was now rebuffed first by British and then by Arab League forces. It was not until October 1963 that a new Iraqi regime formally recognized both Kuwait's independence and, subsequently, its borders, while continuing to press for access to the islands.

IRAN-IRAQ WAR

The Iran-Iraq War of 1980–88 represented a serious threat to Kuwait's security. Kuwait, fearing Iranian hegemony in the region, saw no alternative to providing Iraq with substantial financial support and serving as a vital conduit for military supplies. Iran attacked a Kuwaiti refinery complex in 1981, which inspired subsequent acts of sabotage in 1983 and 1986. In 1985 a member of the underground pro-Iranian Iraqi radical group al-Daʿwah attempted to assassinate the Kuwaiti ruler, Sheikh Jābir al-Aḥmad al-Jābir al-Ṣabāḥ.

In September 1986 Iran began to concentrate its attacks on gulf shipping, largely on Kuwaiti tankers. This led Kuwait to invite both the Soviet Union (with which it had established diplomatic relations in 1963) and the United States to provide protection for its tankers in early 1987. The effect of the war was to promote closer relations with Kuwait's conservative gulf Arab neighbours (Saudi Arabia, Bahrain, Qatar, the United Arab Emirates, and Oman), with whom Kuwait had

Sheikh Jābir al-Aḥmad al-Jābir al-Ṣabāḥ

(b. June 29, 1926, Kuwait city, Kuwait—d. Jan. 15, 2006, Kuwait city)

Sheikh Jābir was a member of the ruling Ṣabāḥ family of Kuwait and that country's emir from 1977 to 2006.

Sheikh Jābir was the third son of Sheikh Aḥmad al-Jābir al-Ṣabāḥ, who ruled Kuwait from 1921 to 1950. Beginning in the late 1940s he held a number of important public positions, including ministries in the government overseeing financial and economic affairs. When Iraq claimed sovereignty over newly independent Kuwait in 1961, he led a delegation to the Arab League to negotiate a settlement. He became prime minister in November 1965, and the following year he was formally designated crown prince and heir apparent to his cousin Sheikh Sạbāḥ al-Sālim al-Ṣabāḥ. By the early 1970s the emir, suffering from poor health, had handed over most of the government operations to Sheikh Jābir, and upon Sheikh Ṣabāḥ's death, on Dec. 31, 1977, Sheikh Jābir became emir.

Early in his rule Sheikh Jābir stressed unity among Arab countries, but he soon found his policies caught in the cross fire of the Iran-Iraq War (1980–88). He was also forced to deal with internal dissent, particularly from Kuwait's Shīʿite minority, and with opposition from the National Assembly. In 1986 he dissolved the parliament and imposed press censorship, which led to periodic protests against the economic and political power of the Ṣabāḥ family. When Iraqi troops invaded Kuwait in August 1990, Sheikh Jābir escaped to Saudi Arabia, where he lived in exile until his return in March 1991. Pressure for reform continued, and in elections held in October 1992 opponents won a majority of seats in the National Assembly. In elections in 1996, however, pro-government forces gained some of the ground they had lost, but in May 1999 Sheikh Jābir once again dissolved the parliament. Although antigovernment sentiment was high in the new parliament, elected in July, the opposition was divided and Sheikh Jābir retained his authority. The emir was noted for his public support for the rights of women (against the wishes of more conservative elements in the country); in 1999 his decree to grant women the right to vote was rejected, but in 2005 women were extended the right to stand and vote in parliamentary elections. In 2001 Sheikh Jābir suffered a stroke and thereafter carried out virtually no public activities.

formed the Gulf Cooperation Council in 1981 in order to develop closer cooperation on economic and security issues. With the end of the Iran-Iraq War in 1988, Iraqi-Kuwaiti relations began to deteriorate. On Aug. 2, 1990, Iraq unexpectedly invaded and conquered the country, precipitating the Persian Gulf War.

THE PERSIAN GULF WAR AND ITS AFTERMATH

Although Iraq advanced several arguments in support of its actions, the basic reasons behind the invasion of Kuwait were the perennial ones that had led earlier Iraqi regimes to seek the same result: control of Kuwait's oil and wealth, the military advantage of frontage on the Persian Gulf, Pan-Arabism under Iraqi leadership, and a way to generate popular support in the wake of its defeat in the Iran-Iraq War. On August 8 Iraq announced its annexation of Kuwait, in spite of condemnations from the United Nations (UN), the major world powers, the Arab League, and the European Community (now the European Union). The vehement anti-Iraqi feelings harboured by virtually all Kuwaitis, in conjunction with diplomatic efforts by the Kuwaiti government-in-exile in Saudi Arabia, did not stop Iraq from harshly imposing its rule on Kuwait.

In mid-January 1991 a coalition of nations, acting under the authority of the UN and led by the United States and

A Kuwaiti woman offers rose water to a U.S. soldier as a sign of welcome on February 27, 1991, after allied forces rolled into Kuwait city. Christophe Simon/AFP/Getty Images

Saudi Arabia, began launching air strikes against Iraqi forces, and five weeks later it conducted a ground assault into Kuwait and Iraq. By late February Kuwait had been liberated from Iraqi control. As hundreds of thousands of Kuwaitis returned from foreign refuges to their homes in May, the full extent of the damage created by the invasion, looting, and war became clear.

The invasion and occupation affected every aspect of Kuwaiti life. More than half the population fled during the war. Although most nationals returned during 1991, many nonnationals, notably the Palestinians, were not permitted to do so. A division emerged between those who had stayed behind in the resistance and those who had fled.

Another developed between the majority pressing for political liberalization (specifically, for parliamentary elections) and the ruling family, whose behaviour in exile had stirred considerable popular disfavour in Kuwait. The government's initial response—instituting martial law and staging show trials—gave way as reconstruction proceeded to a more liberal stance. This led to elections to the National Assembly in 1992, in which Islamic candidates and independent candidates sympathetic to them were successful.

In 1992 a UN commission formally delimited the Iraqi-Kuwaiti border in accordance with a resolution of the UN Security Council passed in April 1991, which had reaffirmed the border's inviolability. The commission's findings were generally favourable to Kuwait, moving the Iraqi border slightly to the north in the area of Safwān and slightly north in the area of the contested Al-Rumaylah oil field and thereby giving Kuwait not only additional oil wells but also part of the Iraqi naval base of Umm Qaṣr. Kuwait accepted the UN's border designation, but Iraq rejected it and continued to voice its claim to Kuwaiti territory.

The survival of the Baʿth regime of Ṣaddām Ḥussein in Iraq spawned an ambient fear among Kuwaitis of a repeat of the events of 1990–91. A tense standoff atmosphere prevailed, exacerbated by Iraqi troop movements along the border, until 2003, when U.S. and British forces launched an invasion of Iraq, largely from bases inside Kuwait. The fall of the Baʿth regime in the Iraq War was greeted with great relief in Kuwait, which offered critical logistic support to the United States and its allies. However, the subsequent occupation of Iraq (and the attraction of some Kuwaitis to the guerrilla insurgency that it produced) led to new political tensions.

Sheikh Sa'd al-'Abd Allāh al-Sālim al-Ṣabāḥ

(b. 1930?, Kuwait—d. May 13, 2008, Kuwait city)

Sheikh Sa'd was a Kuwaiti royal and a member of the ruling Ṣabāḥ family who served in a variety of government posts throughout his career, including prime minister (1978–2003) and, briefly, emir (2006).

Sheikh Sa'd was the eldest son of Sheikh 'Abd Allāh al-Sālim al-Ṣabāḥ, who ruled Kuwait from 1950 to 1965. Sheikh Sa'd trained at the Hendon Police College in London and served as Kuwait's deputy director of police (1959–61) until he joined independent Kuwait's first cabinet. In January 1978 he became prime minister, and the following month he was named crown prince.

In the course of his term as prime minister, Sheikh Sa'd headed a government-in-exile in Saudi Arabia during the 1990–91 Iraqi invasion of Kuwait. When Emir Sheikh Jābir al-Aḥmad al-Jābir al-Ṣabāḥ died on Jan. 15, 2006, Sheikh Sa'd immediately replaced him as emir in accordance with the constitution. A brief power struggle ensued between the two branches of the Ṣabāḥ family, however, and Sheikh Sa'd, then age 76 and in extremely poor health, abdicated after only nine days. (On January 29 his cousin, Prime Minister Sheikh Ṣabāḥ al-Aḥmad al-Jābir al-Ṣabāḥ, was sworn in as emir.)

POLITICAL CONFLICT AND REFORM IN THE EARLY 21ST CENTURY

After suffering a stroke in 2001, Sheikh Jābir al-Aḥmad al-Ṣabāḥ, the ruling emir, carried out few public activities. Following Sheikh Jābir's death in 2006, crown prince Sheikh Sa'd al-'Abd Allāh al-Sālim al-Ṣabāḥ briefly acceded as emir. Although considered too ill to rule, Sheikh Sa'd, who had been crown prince since the late 1970s, sparked a political crisis when he refused to abdicate in favour of

Sheikh Ṣabāḥ al-Aḥmad al-Jābir al-Ṣabāḥ, the country's former foreign minister and already its de facto leader. The succession crisis was resolved after nine days, when the Kuwaiti parliament voted to remove him from office moments before Saʿd himself agreed to abdicate.

Political deadlock and crisis led to frequent legislative elections in Kuwait in the early 21st century, sometimes with less than a year between them. On several occasions, crises precipitated by potential inquiries of government figures and the votes of confidence that would likely ensue led Sheikh Ṣabāḥ to dissolve parliament and call for fresh elections. Although this sidestepped crisis in the short term, it meant that the source of the deadlock was not resolved. At the same time, important political reforms did occur: in 2006 the 25-constituency system in place since 1980 was replaced with a new, five-constituency format meant to discourage voting along tribal lines and to make the buying of votes more difficult. Women won the right to vote in 2005, and in the legislative elections of May 2009 four female candidates became the first women to win seats in parliament. In spite of such advances, observers suggested that the country's patterned encounters with deadlock that only the emir was positioned to resolve would continue to recur unless the Kuwaiti political system were more thoroughly reorganized.

CHAPTER 11

Oman: The Land and Its People

Oman is slightly smaller in area than the country of Poland and is bounded to the southwest by Yemen, to the south and east by the Arabian Sea, to the north by the Gulf of Oman, to the northwest by the United Arab Emirates, and to the west by Saudi Arabia. A small exclave, the Ru'ūs al-Jibāl ("the Mountaintops"), occupies the northern tip of the Musandam Peninsula at the Strait of Hormuz; this territory gives Oman its only frontage on the Persian Gulf. Its offshore territories include Maṣīrah Island to the east and Al-Ḥallāniyyah Island (the largest of the five Khuriyyā Muriyyā Islands) 25 miles (40 km) off the south coast.

Arabs make up more than one-half of the Omani population. In addition, large numbers of ethnic Baloch—who migrated to Oman from Iran and Pakistan over the past several centuries—live in the country, particularly in Al-Bāṭinah. There have long been significant numbers of ethnic Persians and merchants of South Asian ancestry in the Muscat-Maṭraḥ urban area.

RELIEF

Northern Oman is dominated by three physiographic zones. The long, narrow coastal plain known as Al-Bāṭinah stretches along the Gulf of Oman. The high, rugged Ḥajar Mountains extend southeastward, parallel to the gulf coast, from the Musandam Peninsula to a point near Cape Al-Ḥadd at the easternmost tip of the Arabian Peninsula. Much of the range reaches elevations above 4,800 feet (1,500 metres); Mount Al-Akhḍar ("Green Mountain"), which surpasses 10,000 feet (3,000 metres), is the country's highest point. The great central divide of

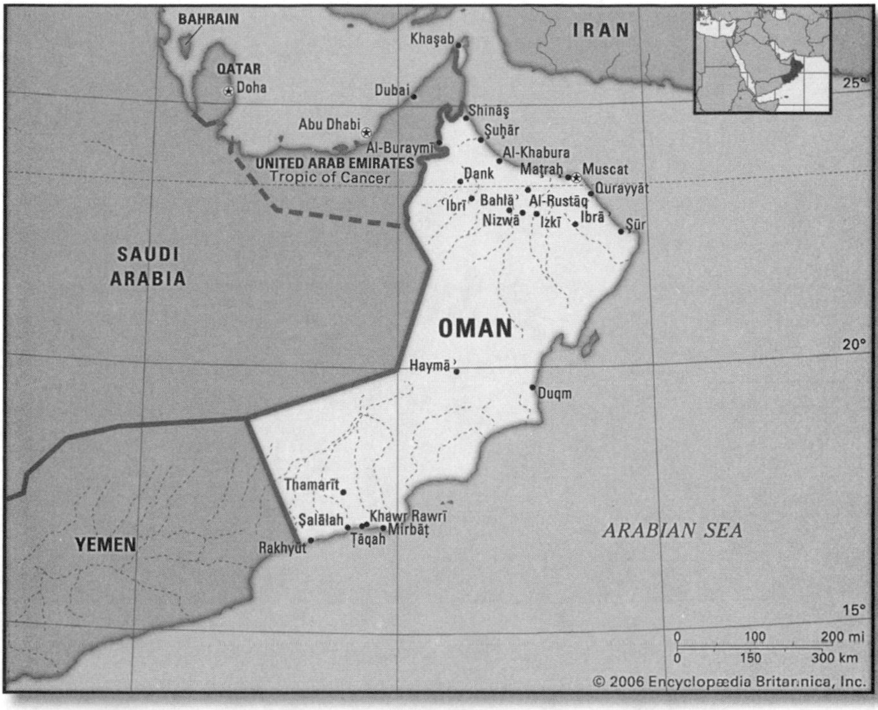

Wadi Samāʾil separates the Ḥajar into a western and an eastern range. An inland plateau falls away to the southwest of the Ḥajar Mountains into the great Rubʿ al-Khali ("Empty Quarter") desert, which the sultanate shares with Saudi Arabia and Yemen. These zones can be further subdivided into several unofficial regions: Al-Bāṭinah; the mountains and associated valleys of the Eastern Ḥajar and Western Ḥajar ranges; the Oman interior area, or Al-Jaww (the central foothills and valleys on the inland side of the Ḥajar Mountains and the historic heartland of Oman); Al-Ẓāhirah (the semidesert plain west of the interior Oman area, next to the United Arab Emirates, including Al-Buraymī oasis); Al-Sharqiyyah (sandy plains lying east of interior Oman behind the Ḥajar Mountains); and Jaʿlān (fronting the Arabian Sea south of Cape Al-Ḥadd).

The southern region of Dhofar (Ẓufār) is separated from the rest of Oman by several hundred miles of open

An Omani woman from the town of Ṣalālah in Dhofar prepares Arabic gum in her incense and gum shop. The region of Dhofar is renowned for delicious gum and special incense. Mohammed Mahjoub AFP/Getty Images

desert. Dhofar's coastal plain is fertile alluvial soil, well watered by the southwest monsoon. Wooded mountain ranges, rising to about 5,000 feet (1,500 metres), form a crescent there behind a long, narrow coastal plain, on which the provincial capital of Ṣalālah is located. Behind the mountains, gravel plains gradually merge northward into the Rub' al-Khali.

DRAINAGE

There are no permanent bodies of fresh water in the country. Intermittent streams are a product of seasonal storms and generally abate quickly. Some effort has been made in recent years to construct dams in an effort to preserve runoff and control flooding.

CLIMATE

The climate is hot and dry in the interior and hot and humid along the coast. Summer temperatures in the capital of Muscat and other coastal locations often climb to 110 °F (43 °C), with high humidity; winters are mild, with lows averaging in the mid-60s F (high 10s C). Temperatures are similar in the interior, although they are more moderate at higher elevations. Dhofar is dominated by the summer monsoon, making Ṣalālah's climate more temperate than that of northern Oman. Precipitation throughout the country is minimal, averaging only about 4 inches (100 mm) per year, although precipitation in the mountains is heavier.

PLANT AND ANIMAL LIFE

Because of the low precipitation, vegetation is sparse except where there is irrigation, which is provided by an

Ḥajar Mountains

The Ḥajar Mountains, in northern Oman, parallel the coast of the Gulf of Oman and stretch in an arc southeastward from the Musandam Peninsula almost to Cape Al-Ḥadd on the extreme northeastern tip of the Arabian Peninsula. From northwest to southeast, the Ḥajar range includes the Ru'ūs al-Jibāl ("the Mountaintops") overlooking the Strait of Hormuz, Al-Ḥajar al-Gharbī (Western Ḥajar), the vast massif of Mount Al-Akhḍar (Green Mountain), the Nakhl Mountains, Al-Ḥajar al-Sharqī (Eastern Ḥajar), and the Banī Jābir Mountains. This range, with its steeper slopes to seaward, reaches above 10,000 feet (3,000 metres) at Mount Al-Akhḍar, although the rest of the range is, on average, a good deal smaller. The Ḥajar Mountains are generally bleak except on Mount Al-Akhḍar, where greater precipitation permits the growth of some alfalfa, date palms, lime bushes, and fruit trees.

Geologically the chain is mostly limestone and is drained by many wadis, such as Wadi Al-Ḥawāsinah, Wadi Samā'il, and Wadi Al-'Udayy. There are many species of wildlife, including leopards and the Arabian tahr, a wild goat not found in the rest of the country. Bowl-like valleys are carved into the northern face of the Ḥajar Mountains by northward-flowing wadis and contain tiny agricultural settlements connected with the coast by graded tracks.

ancient system of water channels known as *aflāj* (singular: *falaj*). The channels often run underground and originate in wells near mountain bases. The *aflāj* collectively were designated a UNESCO World Heritage site in 2006.

Acacia trees form most of what little natural vegetation exists, and the soil is extremely rocky; plant species are protected in nature preserves. The government also protects rare animal species, such as Arabian oryx, Arabian leopards, mountain goats, and loggerhead turtles. However, in 2007 the country's Arabian Oryx Sanctuary, which had been designated a World Heritage site in 1994, became the first site to have its World Heritage status revoked when the government of Oman decided to reduce the size of the sanctuary by 90 percent. Oman's birdlife is extraordinarily diverse and includes such species as glossy ibis, Egyptian vultures, Barbary falcons, and Socotra cormorants.

ETHNIC GROUPS

More than half of Oman's population is Arab. However, large numbers of ethnic Baloch—who migrated to Oman from Iran and Pakistan over the past several centuries—live near the coast in Al-Bāṭinah. The Muscat-Maṭraḥ urban area has long been home to significant numbers of ethnic Persians and to merchants of South Asian ancestry, some of whom also live along Al-Bāṭinah. Notable among the latter are the Liwātiyyah, who originally came from Sindh (now in Pakistan) but have lived in Oman for centuries.

Several large Arab groups predominate along Dhofar's coastal plain. The inhabitants of the Dhofar mountains are known as *jibālī*s, or "people of the mountains." They are ethnically distinct from the coastal Arabs and are thought to be descendants of people from the Yemen highlands.

LANGUAGES

Arabic is the official language, and Modern Standard Arabic is taught in schools. In addition, a number of dialects of vernacular Arabic are spoken, some of which are similar to those spoken in other Persian Gulf states but many of which are not mutually intelligible with those of adjacent regions. The *jibālī*s, for example, speak older dialects of South Arabic. These differ greatly from most other dialects, which are derived from North Arabic (as is Modern Standard Arabic). English, Persian, and Urdu are also

Baloch

The Baloch are a group of tribes speaking the Balochi language and estimated at about five million inhabitants in the province of Balochistān in Pakistan and also neighbouring areas of Iran and Afghanistan. Smaller numbers live in the Persian Gulf region, including in Oman and the United Arab Emirates. In Pakistan the Baloch people are divided into two groups, the Sulaimani and the Makrani, separated from each other by a compact block of Brahui tribes.

The original Baloch homeland probably lay on the Iranian plateau. The Baloch were mentioned in Arabic chronicles of the 10th century CE. The old tribal organization is best preserved among those inhabiting the Sulaimān Mountains. Each tribe (*tuman*) consists of several clans and acknowledges one chief, even though in some *tuman* there are clans in habitual opposition to the chief.

The Baloch are traditionally nomads, but settled agricultural existence is becoming more common; every chief has a fixed residence. The villages are collections of mud or stone huts; on the hills, enclosures of rough stone walls are covered with matting to serve as temporary habitations. The Baloch raise camels, cattle, sheep, and goats and engage in carpet making and embroidery. They engage in agriculture using simple methods and are chiefly Muslim.

spoken, and there are a number of Swahili-speaking Omanis born in Zanzibar and elsewhere in East Africa who returned to Oman after 1970. Various South Asian languages are also spoken.

RELIGION

The overwhelming majority of Omanis are Muslims. The Ibāḍī branch of Islam, a moderate Khārijite group, claims the most adherents. In belief and ritual, Ibāḍism is close to Sunni Islam (the major branch of Islam), differing in its emphasis on an elected, rather than a hereditary, imam as the spiritual and temporal leader of the Ibāḍī community. Non-Ibāḍī Arabs and the Baloch are mostly Sunnis. Those in the South Asian communities are mainly Shīʿite, although a few are Hindus.

SETTLEMENT PATTERNS

The population of Oman is primarily urban but has a number of traditional rural settlements. These are typically located near the foothills of the Ḥajar Mountains, where the *aflāj* provide irrigation. In addition to small villages, a number of sizable towns, including Nizwā, Bahlā', Izkī, and ʿIbrī, are found on the inland, or southwestern, side of the Western Ḥajar. Coastal Al-Bāṭinah provides opportunities for fishing, as well as irrigated cultivation, and is therefore more densely populated, with such major towns as Shināṣ, Ṣuḥār, Al-Khābūrah, Al-Maṣnaʿah, and Barkā'. Approximately one-fourth of the population lives in Al-Bāṭinah. Al-Rustāq, ʿAwābī, and Nakhl are principal settlements on Al-Bāṭinah's side of the Western Ḥajar.

The twin cities of Muscat and Maṭraḥ lie at the eastern end of Al-Bāṭinah; both are ancient ports, but they have merged to become an important metropolitan centre. Al-Bāṭinah is the country's most densely populated area. To the east the only major town is Ṣūr, a well-protected port that is still a notable centre for fishing and boatbuilding. The central region of interior Oman consists of irrigated valleys lying between the mountains and the desert and is also one of the more densely populated areas. Some of Dhofar's residents are concentrated in towns along the coast, while others are seminomadic cattle herders in the mountains. A small nomadic population inhabits the inland plateaus along the Rubʿ al-Khali. Khaṣab is the only significant town in the sparsely populated Musandam Peninsula.

Khārijite

The earliest Islamic sect, which traces its beginning to a religio-political controversy over the caliphate in the 600s, is the Khārijite sect (Arabic: Khawārij).

The Khārijites' held that the judgment of God could only be expressed through the free choice of the entire Muslim community. They insisted that anyone could be elected caliph (that is, head of the Muslim community) if he possessed the necessary qualifications, chiefly religious piety and moral purity. A caliph may be deposed upon the commission of any major sin. The Khārijites thus set themselves against the legitimist claims (to the caliphate) of the tribe of Quraysh (among the Sunnis) and of 'Alī's descendants (among the Shī'ites). As proponents of the democratic principle, the Khārijites drew to themselves many who were dissatisfied with the existing political and religious authorities. The Khārijites' constant harassment of the various Muslim governments was less a matter of personal enmity than a practical exercise of their religious beliefs.

Besides their democratic theory of the caliphate, the Khārijites were known for their puritanism and fanaticism. Any Muslim who committed a major sin was considered an apostate. Luxury, music, games, and concubinage without the consent of wives were forbidden. Intermarriage and relations with other Muslims were strongly discouraged. The doctrine of justification by faith without works was rejected, and literal interpretation of the Qur'ān was insisted upon.

Within the Khārijite movement the Azāriqah of Basra were the most extreme subsect, separating themselves from the Muslim community and declaring death to all sinners and their families. The more moderate subsect of the Ibāḍiyyah, however, survived into modern times in North Africa, Oman, and Zanzibar.

DEMOGRAPHIC TRENDS

Oman has one of the highest birth rates among the Persian Gulf states; this birth rate—combined with a relatively low death rate—has given the country a rate of natural increase that well exceeds the world average. Life expectancy averages about 73 years for men and 75 years for women. The population, on the whole, is very young: more than one-third of the population is under age 15, and nearly three-fourths are under age 30.

Since 1970, increasing numbers of foreigners have come to reside in the country, particularly in the capital. These include Western businesspeople, as well as government advisers, army officers, and labourers from the Indian subcontinent, the Philippines, and other Asian countries. Since the 1980s the government has followed a policy termed "Omanization," to reduce the country's dependence on foreign labour and increase employment opportunities for Omani citizens.

CHAPTER 12

The Omani Economy

Oman is a rural, agricultural country, and fishing and overseas trading are important to the coastal populations. Oil in commercial quantities was discovered in Oman in 1964 and was first exported in 1967. Subsequently the production and export of petroleum rapidly came to dominate the country's economy. Oil revenues continue to represent a significant proportion of both the gross domestic product (GDP) and the government's income.

In anticipation of the eventual depletion of oil reserves, the government in 1996 initiated a plan for the post-oil era that focused on developing the country's natural gas resources to fuel domestic industry and for export in the form of liquefied natural gas (LNG). Oman also sought to diversify and privatize its economy in addition to implementing its policy of Omanization. By the end of the 1990s, the privatization plan had advanced further than those in the other states of the Gulf Cooperation Council (GCC)—Kuwait, Qatar, Saudi Arabia, Bahrain, and the United Arab Emirates. Notable features of the program included expanding the country's stock market, selling several government-owned companies, and creating a more liberal investment environment. The country's development has been aided in part by the GCC.

AGRICULTURE AND FISHING

Agriculture is practiced mainly for subsistence and employs less than one-tenth of the labour force. The *falaj* irrigation system has long supported a three-tiered crop approach (i.e., three crops raised at different heights within the same plot), with date palms above; lime, banana, or mango trees in the middle level; and alfalfa (lucerne),

Falaj *in a date grove on Mount Al-Akhḍar, Oman.* A.C. Waltham/Robert Harding Picture Library

wheat, and sorghum at ground level. Vegetables, melons, tomatoes, bananas, and dates are the country's most significant crops. Limes that are grown in the interior oases are traded for fish from coastal areas as well as exported abroad. Grapes, walnuts, peaches, and other fruits are cultivated on the high mountain plateaus; Dhofar also produces coconuts and papayas. Although agricultural production meets some local needs, most food must be imported. Many rural families keep goats, and Oman is well known for camel breeding. Cattle are raised throughout the mountainous areas of Dhofar.

The emigration of a large portion of the workforce to neighbouring countries before 1970 allowed fields to lie fallow and the irrigation systems to decay. In an attempt to reduce the country's dependence on food imports, the government has sought to stimulate agricultural production by establishing research stations and model farms along Al-Bāṭinah's coast and in Dhofar, as well as date-processing plants at Al-Rustāq and Nizwā. The government has also encouraged the development of commercial fishing by providing boats and motors, cold-storage facilities, and transportation. In the 1990s the United States provided Oman with aid to help develop its potentially large fisheries in the Gulf of Oman and the Arabian Sea.

RESOURCES AND POWER

Crude oil production was high throughout the oil boom of the 1970s, and declining oil prices in the 1980s prompted the government to further increase production in an attempt to maintain revenue. This policy, however, was reversed in 1986 when Oman followed the lead of the Organization of Petroleum Exporting Countries (OPEC) and sought to sustain price levels through production cuts aimed at diminishing world oil supplies. Production again increased in the 1990s, and in the early 21st century the country's oil production was roughly three times the rates of the 1970s. Oman, however, still remains far behind the ranks of the world's largest oil exporters.

Several copper mines and a smelter were opened in the early 1980s at an ancient mining site near Ṣuḥār, but production levels have diminished considerably. Chromite is also mined in small quantities. Coal deposits at Al-Kāmil have been explored for potential exploitation and use, especially to generate electricity. Exploration projects that began in the mid-1980s to uncover more unassociated natural gas have proved successful, and pipelines were constructed from the gas fields at Yibāl to Muscat and Ṣuḥār and to Izkī. By the late 1990s the known natural gas reserves were double those of less than a decade earlier. A facility for the liquefaction of natural gas was opened in Qalhāt, and in 2000 Oman began exporting LNG.

MANUFACTURING

Oman's non-petroleum manufactures include non-metallic mineral products, foods, and chemicals and chemical products. Industrial development, virtually nonexistent before 1970, began with a change of government that ended years of isolation in Oman. It has since been oriented toward projects that improve the country's infrastructure, such as electric generators, desalinization complexes, and cement plants outside Muscat and Ṣalālah. Successive government five-year plans have stressed private-sector development as well as joint ventures with the government. Meanwhile, the practice of traditional handicrafts (weaving, pottery, boatbuilding, and gold and silver work) has been declining.

FINANCE

The Central Bank of Oman is the country's main monetary and banking regulatory body. Founded in 1974, it issues and regulates the national currency, the Omani rial, manages the government's accounts, and acts as lender of last resort. The country has commercial and development banks, and a number of foreign banks operate there. A stock exchange, the Muscat Securities Exchange, was opened in 1988.

TRADE

Crude oil, refined petroleum, and natural gas account for most exports, while imports consist mainly of machinery and transport equipment, basic manufactured goods, and foodstuffs. Some manufactured products are also exported. Among the country's major trading partners are China, Japan, South Korea, and the United Arab Emirates. In 2000 Oman became a member of the World Trade Organization.

SERVICES

Services, including public administration and defense, account for roughly one-fifth of the value of GDP and employ some two-fifths of the workforce. In spite of the country's frequent balance-of-payment deficits, defense spending consistently constitutes a significant portion of the total budget. The tourist trade contributes only a small fraction of Oman's GDP; however, the government has been promoting the sector more aggressively in an attempt to further diversify the economy.

LABOUR AND TAXATION

Before 1970 thousands of Omanis left the country to find work in nearby oil-producing states; later foreigners came to work in Oman as oil production increased. Non-Omanis still constitute more than one-half of the labour force; far more foreign-born men are employed than are Omani men. Women constitute a small but growing portion of the workforce. There are no trade unions or associations in Oman, though the government has created consultative committees to mediate grievances. Strikes are forbidden. The workweek is Saturday through Wednesday.

Personal income and property are not taxed in Oman. Corporate tax rates are determined by the level of Omani ownership; the greater the percentage of Omani ownership, the lower the rate of taxation. In the late 1990s,

Ṣalālah

Ṣalālah is a town in southern Oman, situated on the coast of the Arabian Sea. The town is located in the only part of the Arabian Peninsula touched by the Indian Ocean monsoon and thus is verdant during the summer. Ṣalālah is the historic centre of Dhofar, famous in ancient times as a source of frankincense, and was described by Marco Polo in the 13th century as a prosperous city. Although it declined in wealth and importance in succeeding centuries, Ṣalālah did not come under the rule of the sultans of Oman until the 1800s. From 1932 until he was deposed in July 1970, Sultan Saʿīd ibn Taymūr ruled the country, then called Muscat and Oman, from Ṣalālah.

After an insurrection centred in Dhofar ended in 1975, the government began to develop the Ṣalālah area. Projects included a large modern hospital and a hotel. The town's airport was upgraded to international standards, and a paved road was built linking Ṣalālah with the north. In 2006 a free-trade zone was established in Ṣalālah, which is now a major shipping hub. The town trades in agricultural products from the surrounding coastal plain.

however, the government lowered rates on foreign-owned firms to encourage investment. Oil companies are taxed separately by the Ministry of Petroleum and Minerals.

TRANSPORTATION AND TELECOMMUNICATION

Oman has several ports, most notably Port Qābūs in Maṭraḥ, Ṣalālah (formerly known as Port Raysūt), and Al-Faḥl, all of which were built after 1970; in 2004 work to upgrade and expand the industrial port at Ṣuḥār was completed. Ṣalālah underwent major renovations and in 1998 opened as one of the world's largest container terminals; the port is considered by international shippers to be the preferred off-loading site in the Persian Gulf. Significant intercoastal trade is carried on by traditional wooden dhows. The two principal airports are located at Al-Sīb, about 19 miles (30 km) from Muscat, and at Ṣalālah. The government also operates the national carrier, Oman Air, both domestically and internationally. Since 1970 a modern network of asphalt and gravel roads has been built up from virtually nothing to link all the country's main settlements; more than two-fifths of the country's road network is paved. The country has no railroads.

Government-owned Omantel (formerly known as General Telecommunications Organization) is Oman's primary telecommunications provider. During the 1990s it instituted plans that increased the number of phone lines, expanded the fibre-optic network, and introduced digital technology. The Internet became available in 1997, with Omantel as the official provider. The use of cell phones increased dramatically after Omantel lost its monopoly on the mobile phone market in 2004. Satellite links provide much of the country's international communications.

CHAPTER 13

Omani Government and Society

Oman is governed by a monarchy (sultanate) with two advisory bodies. The sultan is the head of state, and, although he also acts as the prime minister, he may appoint one if he chooses. The sultan is assisted by a Council of Ministers (Majlis al-Wuzarā'), the members of which he typically appoints from among Muscat merchants, informal representatives of interior tribes, and Dhofaris.

The Consultative Assembly, formed by the sultan in 1981, was replaced in 1991 by a Consultative Council (Majlis al-Shūrā), members of which were at first appointed and later elected from several dozen districts (*wilāyāt*); women from a few constituencies were given the right to serve on the council. In 1996 the sultan announced the establishment of the Basic Law of the State, the country's first written constitution, which outlined a new system of government that included a bicameral legislature, the Council of Oman. In addition, it clarified the succession process and extended the right to serve to all Omani women. The Council of Oman consists of the Consultative Council as its lower chamber and, as the upper chamber, a new Council of State (Majlis al-Dawlah).

Local Government

The country is divided administratively into regions (*minṭaqāt*) and governorates (*muḥāfaẓat*), each of which contains a number of districts (*wilāyāt*). Local governance is carried out by a combination of traditional *wālī*s (representatives of the sultan) and by more recently established municipal councils.

JUSTICE

Oman has Islamic courts, based on the Ibāḍī interpretation of the Sharīʿah (Islamic law), which handle personal status cases. There are also civil, criminal, and commercial courts that are organized into courts of first instance, appeals courts, and a Supreme Court, which is chaired by the sultan. In addition, there are some specialized courts.

POLITICAL PROCESS

There are no political parties. Elections to the Consultative Council have been held since 1994. At first, voting was limited to individuals chosen by the government; the pool of eligible voters was 50,000 in 1994 and 175,000 in 2000. Universal suffrage for citizens at least 21 years old was implemented in 2003. Members of the Council of State are appointed by the sultan.

SECURITY

As a proportion of the GDP, Oman's military expenditures are the world's highest. The Sultan's Armed Forces, formed in 1958 from several smaller regiments, has grown since 1970 to more than 40,000 personnel, spurred in part by a rebellion in Dhofar in 1964–75. Most personnel are in the army, but Oman also maintains a small air force and navy and fields some of the most sophisticated military equipment available. The sultan is the commander in chief of the armed forces. The military has traditionally relied heavily on foreign advisers and officers, mostly British, and the United States and the United Kingdom have occasionally maintained a small military presence in the country.

Omani women in traditional dress show off their horseriding skills while on horseback during a show at the al-Feleij track in Muscat on April 17, 2008. Mohammed Mahjoub AFP/Getty Images

HEALTH AND WELFARE

The post-1970 government improved health care throughout the country and instituted a free national health service. The new regime built hospitals, health centres, and dispensaries and equipped mobile medical teams to serve remote areas. Government spending has increased for health services, social security, and welfare.

HOUSING

The move to towns and the return of Omanis abroad in the 1970s led to a severe housing shortage. In 1973 the government established a program that built homes for those on limited incomes. The Oman Housing Bank was established in 1998 to finance the purchase, construction, or renovation of residential property for those with lower incomes. Traditional housing in Al-Bāṭinah often consists of palm-frond huts, in contrast to the mud-brick structures of the interior. More recently, however, such homes have largely been replaced by more modern dwellings of concrete, though elements of traditional regional architecture have been retained.

EDUCATION

Education has expanded dramatically since 1970, when only three primary schools existed and few girls received any schooling. Almost three-fourths of elementary-school-age and almost four-fifths of secondary-school-age children are now enrolled. Education is provided free to all Omanis but is not mandatory. More than four-fifths of Oman's adult population is literate; there has been a substantial increase in the number of literate women (although female literacy lags behind that of men). The country's national university, Sultan Qaboos University, was opened in Muscat in 1986. Oman also has several private colleges.

CHAPTER 14

Omani Cultural Life

Oman is a tribal society, although tribal influence is gradually declining. Its predominantly Ibāḍī Muslim population observes social customs that—though still conservative by Western standards—are markedly less strict than those of neighbouring Saudi Arabia. (The consumption of alcoholic beverages, for instance, is illegal for Omani citizens but is permissible for visitors in licensed dining establishments.) Women in particular have enjoyed relatively more freedom in Oman than elsewhere on the Arabian Peninsula. Social interaction remains largely segregated by gender, however, and most Omani women—particularly those in rural areas—dress in a conservative, time-honoured fashion. Traditional attire for women, although varying slightly from region to region, is characterized by brightly coloured fabrics and jeweled adornments and consists of a dress (*thawb*) over loose-fitting slacks (*sirwāl*). A long, flowing scarf known as a *liḥāf* (or generically as *ḥijāb*) covers the head. Similarly, most Omani men wear the *dishdashah*, or *thawb*, a traditional woven cotton robe, and male headgear consists of a light turban of cotton or wool, known as a *muzzar*. Many men continue to carry a short, broad, curved, and often highly ornate dagger known as a *khanjar* (sometimes called a *janbiyyah* or *jambiya*), which is worn tucked in the front waistband.

Mealtime serves as the centre of most social gatherings. The typical Omani meal consists of rice, spiced lamb or fish, dates, and coffee or tea. Incense—notably frankincense, which is native to Oman—is burned at the end of the meal.

Omanis observe the standard Islamic holidays, including the two *ʿīd*s (festivals), ʿĪd al-Fiṭr and ʿĪd al-Aḍḥā, as well as several secular holidays, such as National Day (celebrating the expulsion of the Portuguese in the 17th century) and the ruling sultan's birthday.

THE ARTS

Omani artisans are renowned for woodcarving, weaving, and silver- and goldsmithing and for the manufacture of

An Omani vendor holds a dagger at his shop at the Maṭraḥ souk in Muscat on January 16, 2009. Karim Jaafar/AFP/Getty Images

daggers and swords. Their handiworks are among the many items that may be found at the souk, or market, of Muscat, a thriving centre of popular culture. The Ministry of National Heritage and Culture is charged with preserving historic buildings, excavating archaeological sites, and supporting such traditional crafts as weaving and the crafting of silver and gold jewelry. It also promotes Omani literature and has printed an encyclopaedia of Omani heritage. The annual Muscat International Book Fair promotes books from throughout the Arabic-speaking world.

Just as attempts have been made to preserve much of traditional society in the midst of development, traditional elements of architecture have been incorporated into new buildings; the result is that Oman's cities feel at once contemporary and ancient. The country's restored forts and castles, the subject of several documentary films, are among the most important historic sites in Oman. Architecturally, particularly significant structures include a series of forts guarding Muscat's harbour and several strategic strongholds guarding the interior, most of which date to the 17th century. The most noteworthy of these is Bahlā Fort, a stone and mud-brick edifice that dates to the pre-Islamic era and was designated a World Heritage site in 1987. Other sites in Oman enjoying this distinction are the prehistoric settlements at Bāt, Al-Khutm, and Al-ʿAyn (designated in 1988); the country's *aflāj* irrigation systems (designated in 2006); and the Frankincense Trail (designated in 2000), which consists of a series of stops along the ancient trade route.

CULTURAL INSTITUTIONS

Oman Museum (founded 1974), located outside Muscat, is the country's foremost cultural repository; it chronicles the country's history and includes exhibits on Islam.

Oman has a long history as a trading nation. The Jewel of Muscat, *a reconstructed replica of a ninth century Omani sailing ship, sails into the harbour of Galle, Sri Lanka, on April 19, 2010. The ship, built in a traditional design without nails and sewn together with coconut fibers, left Oman on February 15 to re-enact the old trade routes used by Arab traders, with its final port of call in Singapore.* Lakruwan Wanniarachchi/AFP/Getty Images

The history of the Omani army is the focus of the Armed Forces Museum (1988). Other institutions include the National Museum (1978), Natural History Museum (1983), Children's Museum (1990), and Bait Nadir, a converted 18th-century residence that now houses Omani art and traditional items, including jewelry, silverware, pottery, and woodcarvings. The Royal Oman Symphony Orchestra was formed in the late 1980s and has performed with the BBC Philharmonic Orchestra.

SPORTS AND RECREATION

Dhow racing is a popular traditional sport, as is camel racing. Bedouin still train most of the camels used for the races, which take place on racetracks and on makeshift courses in the open desert. Arabian horses have long been bred in the country, and racing is a popular spectator sport. Falconry is practiced by the wealthy elite. More-modern activities include sandsurfing and waterskiing; football (soccer) and rugby are also widely played. Oman made its first Olympic appearance at the 1984 Summer Games, but the country has not competed at the Winter Games. Omani athletes also participate in the quadrennial Asian Games.

MEDIA AND PUBLISHING

In addition to state-run newspapers, several independent Arabic- and English-language newspapers are published on a daily and weekly basis. Although the government guarantees freedom of the press, it has the right to censor all domestic and imported publications that it considers politically or culturally offensive. The television station is state-run, and radio stations broadcast in both Arabic and English.

CHAPTER 15

Oman: Past and Present

Three principal themes highlight the history of Oman: the tribal nature of its society, the traditional Ibāḍī imamate form of government, and its maritime tradition. Archaeological evidence of civilization in Oman dates to about the 3rd millennium BCE, but Persian colonization prior to the 1st century CE established the *falaj* irrigation system, which has since sustained Omani agriculture and civilization.

The history of the Dhofar region followed a separate path. Ancient South Arabian kingdoms controlled the production of frankincense there from the 1st century CE. The province thus remained culturally and politically linked to South Arabia until it was absorbed into the Āl Bū Saʿīd state in the 19th century.

THE OMANI TRIBAL SYSTEM

The origins of the Omani tribal system can be traced to the immigration of Arab groups from South Arabia into the Jaʿlān region during the 2nd century CE. These groups subsequently moved northward into the Persian-controlled area of Māzūn in Oman, where they confronted other tribes from the northwest. Arab dominance over the country began with the introduction of Islam in the 7th century.

THE IBĀḌĪ IMAMATE

The Ibāḍī imamate, which arrived in the mid-8th century, unified Oman politically. The country's mountains and geographic isolation provided a refuge for the Ibāḍīs

(Ibāḍiyyah), who proceeded to convert the leading tribal clans to their sect. The new Ibāḍī state was headed by an elected imam who served as both temporal and religious leader of the community. The selection of a new imam was determined by an agreement made among the religious leaders and the heads of the major groups, particularly the leaders of the two major tribal confederations that came to be known as the Ghāfirīs and the Hināwīs.

A recurring pattern began to develop during the decline of the First Imamate, which reached its heyday in the 9th century. Elected imams tended to give way to hereditary dynasties, which then collapsed as a result of family disputes and the resurgence of Ibāḍī ideals.

THE MARITIME TRADITION

Maritime trade also contributed to dynastic decline. Virtually cut off from the rest of the Arabian Peninsula by vast deserts, Omani sailors traveled the waters of the Indian Ocean and ranged as far as China by the 15th century. This maritime tendency was strongest when tribal dynasties moved their capitals from the Ibāḍī interior to the coast and focused their attention on acquiring territory elsewhere in the Gulf of Oman, along the Arabian Sea, and on the coast of East Africa.

OMAN SINCE *C.* 1500

En route to India, the Portuguese sacked Muscat in 1507 and soon controlled the entire coast. More than a century later the Yaʿrubid dynasty drove the Portuguese from the Omani coast, recapturing Muscat in 1650 and then occupying Portuguese settlements in the Persian Gulf and East African coastal regions. Their empire eventually crumbled

Old Portuguese fort in Muscat harbour, Oman. Kofod/FPG

in a civil war over the succession of the imam in the early 18th century, enabling the Persian ruler Nādir Shāh to invade the country in 1737.

RESTORATION OF OMANI RULE

Aḥmad ibn Saʿīd, the governor of Ṣuḥār, drove out the Persian invaders and was elected imam in 1749, thus establishing the Āl Bū Saʿīd dynasty that still rules Oman today. Under the rule of his grandson, Saʿīd ibn Sulṭān (1806/07–56), Oman reasserted control over Zanzibar, but upon his death the Āl Bū Saʿīd empire was split between two sons: one received Zanzibar, which remained under Āl Bū Saʿīd rule until 1964, and the other ruled Oman.

The fortunes of the Āl Bū Saʿīd state in Oman declined throughout the second half of the 19th century. However, the dynasty remained in power with the help of the British, who supported the Āl Bū Saʿīd sultans in Muscat against periodic revivals of the Ibāḍī imamate in the interior.

Periodic Civil Unrest

Tribal attacks in the name of the imam were made on Muscat and Maṭraḥ in 1895 and 1915. In 1920 the Agreement of Al-Sīb was negotiated by the British between the tribal leaders and Sultan Taymūr ibn Fayṣal, who reigned in 1913–32. By its terms, the sultan recognized the autonomy but not the sovereignty of the Omani interior.

The interior remained autonomous until 1954, when Muḥammad al-Khalīlī, who had ruled as imam since 1920, died. His weak successor, Ghālib, was influenced by his brother Ṭālib and by a prominent tribal leader, Sulaymān ibn Ḥimyār; the three set out to create an independent state, enlisting Saudi Arabia's support against Sultan Saʿīd ibn Taymūr. Clashes between the sultan's forces and those of the imam continued throughout the 1950s. The authority of the sultan was subsequently restored after a regiment led by British officers moved into the Omani interior and suppressed an imamate rebellion. Remnants of the imamate's supporters, however, held strongholds in the Mount Al-Akhḍar massif of the Western Ḥajar until they were forced to surrender in early 1959.

In the early 1960s another threat to the sultanate emerged in the Dhofar region. Sultan Saʿīd ibn Taymūr had moved to Ṣalālah permanently in 1958. The mountain *jibālī*s began to rebel openly against Sultan Saʿīd's oppressive practices. The Marxist Popular Front for the Liberation of the Occupied Arab Gulf (later called the Popular Front for the Liberation of Oman; PFLO) gained control of the growing rebellion by the late 1960s with the aid of the People's Republic of China, the Soviet

Union, Marxist South Yemen (which had achieved independence from the British in late 1967), and Iraq.

Contemporary Oman

The Dhofar rebellion led to a palace coup on July 23, 1970, when Sultan Saʿīd was overthrown by his son, Qaboos bin Said. Qaboos, who had been trained in Britain at the Royal Military Academy Sandhurst, quickly reversed his father's policy of isolation and began to develop and modernize Oman. Sultan Qaboos appointed the country's first official cabinet and took steps toward building a modern government structure. Qaboos served as prime minister after his uncle, Ṭāriq ibn Taymūr, resigned the position, and he also held the post of minister of defense and foreign affairs. At the same time, the rebellion in Dhofar continued. With British personnel and equipment, Jordanian and Iranian troops, and financial assistance from the United Arab Emirates and Saudi Arabia, the rebellion was finally crushed in December 1975.

Oman joined the Arab League and the United Nations in 1971, but it did not become a member of OPEC or the smaller Organization of Arab Petroleum Exporting Countries. Oman was one of six founding members of the Gulf Cooperation Council, established in 1981 to promote economic, political, and security cooperation among its members. It has been closely linked to Britain since the early 19th century, and relations with the United States, established in 1833 by a treaty of friendship, have grown closer since the 1970s. Although Sultan Qaboos was vocal in his opposition to the Iraq War that began in 2003, Oman remained a significant ally of the United States and continued to provide important military support for U.S. operations in the Persian Gulf region and in Afghanistan. After Oman joined the World Trade Organization in

Qaboos bin Said

(b. Nov. 18, 1940, Muscat and Oman)

Qaboos bin Said (also spelled Qābūs ibn Sa'īd) is the sultan of Oman (1970–).

Qaboos, a member of Oman's Āl Bū Sa'īd dynasty, was educated at Bury Saint Edmunds, Suffolk, England, and at the Royal Military Academy, Sandhurst. He was called home in 1965 by his father, Sa'īd ibn Taymūr, who kept his son a virtual prisoner for six years while maintaining his subjects in a state of relative underdevelopment in spite of the country's growing oil revenues.

In 1970 Qaboos took over the palace in a coup with British support and exiled his father. He immediately undertook a range of ambitious modernization projects, including constructing roads, hospitals, schools, communications systems, and industrial and port facilities. He abrogated his father's moralistic laws and established a Council of Ministers (cabinet) and first one and later two consultative bodies. Political power, however, remained concentrated in the royal family, although Qaboos's regime gradually allowed other Omanis (including women) to participate in the government. He also made considerable progress in ending Oman's isolation by joining the Arab League and the United Nations, aligning his country with the moderate Arab powers.

2000, it made greater efforts to liberalize its markets and improve its standing in the global economy.

Oman's location has made the country pivotal in maintaining the security of traffic through the Strait of Hormuz. Oman attempted to maintain neutrality in the Iran-Iraq War (1980–88), although the sultanate permitted Western military units to use its facilities after Iraq's invasion of Kuwait in 1990, and an Omani regiment participated in the Persian Gulf War (1990–91). Border agreements were signed with Saudi Arabia in 1990 and with Yemen in 1992;

in addition, an agreement was reached on unsettled parts of the boundary with the United Arab Emirates in 1999.

Domestically, 2000 marked the initiation of a program of Omanization, which was meant to reduce the country's reliance on expatriate labour. A 2005 call by Sultan Qaboos for Omanis to focus on having smaller families was in part meant to help curtail the size of the country's labour force overall and ultimately minimize unemployment.

While the right to vote had previously been vested in a select number of individuals, particularly intellectuals and tribal leaders, in 2003 universal voting rights were extended for the first time to all Omanis over the age of 21. Political stability in Oman remains tied to the ability of the country to diversify economically beyond its ongoing dependence on oil, though. Oil reserves are dwindling, and at current consumption levels, they are not expected to last for more than two decades. Governmental plans to reduce oil dependency to less than 10 percent of the country's GDP in the next decade include the development of tourism, real estate, investment, and renewable energy initiatives.

At the end of the first decade of the 21st century, Sultan Qaboos reached his 70th birthday. With no children, and having publically designated no heir, it was unclear how succession would be managed and where political power would lie following the end of Qaboos's rule.

CHAPTER 16

Qatar: The Land and Its People

The Qatar peninsula, slightly smaller than the U.S. state of Connecticut, is about 100 miles (160 km) from north to south, 50 miles (80 km) from east to west, and is generally rectangular in shape. It shares a border with eastern Saudi Arabia where the peninsula connects to the mainland and is north and west of the United Arab Emirates. The island country of Bahrain lies some 25 miles (40 km) northwest of Qatar. A territorial dispute with Bahrain was resolved in 2001, when the International Court of Justice awarded the Ḥawār Islands (just off the coast of Qatar) to Bahrain and gave Qatar sovereignty over Janān Island and the ruined fortress-town of Al-Zubārah (on the Qatari mainland). That year Qatar also signed a final border demarcation agreement with Saudi Arabia.

Qatari citizens are a minority population in their country: they account for only about one-seventh of the total population. The Qatari economy is dependent on large quantities of foreign workers, most of whom originate from other Arab countries and from Pakistan, India, and Iran. More than one-tenth of the population is Palestinian.

Relief and Drainage

Most of Qatar's area is flat, low-lying desert, which rises from the east to a central limestone plateau. Hills rise to about 130 feet (40 metres) along the western and northern coasts, and Abū al-Bawl Hill (335 feet [103 m]) is the country's highest point. Sand dunes and salt flats, or *sabkhah*s, are the chief topographical features of the southern and southeastern sectors. Qatar has more than 350 miles (560 km) of coastline; its border with Saudi Arabia is some

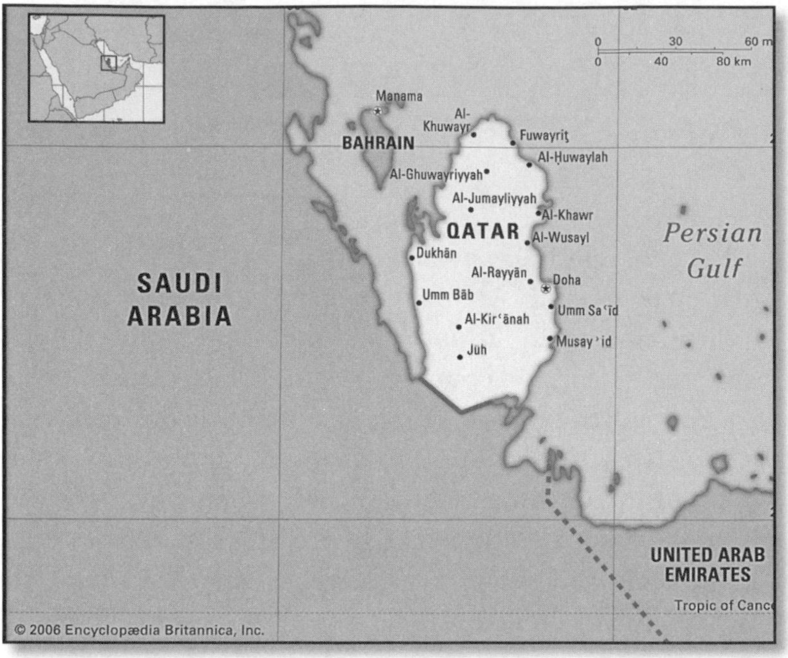

37 miles (60 km) long. There are no permanent bodies of fresh water.

SOILS

Soils in Qatar are marked by a small degree of organic material and are generally calcareous and agriculturally unproductive. Windblown sand dunes are common, and soil distribution over bedrock is light and uneven. Soil salinity is high in coastal regions and in agricultural regions where poor regulation of irrigation has led to increased salinity.

CLIMATE

The climate is hot and humid from June to September, with daytime temperatures reaching the mid-120s F (low 50s C). The spring and fall months—April, May, October,

Sabkhah

*Sabkhah*s are saline flats or salt-crusted depressions, commonly found along the coasts of North Africa and the Arabian Peninsula. *Sabkhah*s are generally bordered by sand dunes and have soft, poorly cemented but impermeable floors, due to periodic flooding and evaporation. Concentration of seawater and capillary discharge of groundwater result in deposits of gypsum, calcite, and aragonite. Most *sabkhah*s are thought to have once been small sea inlets and are akin to basins in which evaporites formed in the geological past.

and November—are temperate, averaging in the mid-60s F (high 10s C), and the winters are slightly cooler. Precipitation is scarce, with less than 3 inches (75 mm) falling annually (generally in winter).

PLANT AND ANIMAL LIFE

Vegetation is found only in the north, where the country's irrigated farming areas are located and where desert plants blossom briefly during the spring rains. Fauna is limited, and the government has implemented a program to protect the Arabian oryx, Qatar's national animal.

ETHNIC GROUPS AND LANGUAGES

Qatar was originally settled by Bedouin nomads from the central part of the Arabian Peninsula. Qatari citizens, however, constitute only a small portion—roughly one-seventh—of the total population today, as mentioned previously. Economic growth beginning in the 1970s created an economy dependent on foreign workers—mostly from other Arab countries and from Pakistan,

A minaret and houses in the capital city of Doha, Qatar. © Peter Vine

India, and Iran—who now far outnumber nationals. Few nomads remain.

Arabic is the official language, and most Qataris speak a dialect of Gulf Arabic similar to that spoken in surrounding states. Modern Standard Arabic is taught in schools, and English is commonly used. Among the large expatriate population, Persian and Urdu are often spoken.

RELIGION

Islam is the official religion, and Qataris are largely Sunni Muslims. There is a small Shīʿite minority. The ruling Āl Thānī (Thānī family) adheres to the same Wahhābī interpretation of Islam as the rulers of Saudi Arabia, though not as strictly. Women, for example, have greater freedom in Qatar than in Saudi Arabia.

Wahhābī

Wahhābīs are members of the Muslim puritan movement founded by Muḥammad ibn ʿAbd al-Wahhāb in the 18th century in Najd, central Arabia, and adopted in 1744 by the Saʿūd family.

The political fortunes of the Wahhābī were immediately allied to those of the Saʿūdī dynasty. By the end of the 18th century, they had brought all of Najd under their control, attacked Karbalāʾ, Iraq, a holy city of the Shīʿite branch of Islam, and occupied Mecca and Medina in western Arabia. The Ottoman sultan brought an end to the first Wahhābī empire in 1818, but the sect revived under the leadership of the Saʿūdī Fayṣal I. The empire was then somewhat restored until once again destroyed at the end of the 19th century by the Rashīdīs of northern Arabia. The activities of Ibn Saʿūd in the 20th century eventually led to the creation of the Kingdom of Saudi Arabia in 1932 and assured the Wahhābī religious and political dominance on the Arabian Peninsula.

Wahhābīs call themselves al-Muwaḥḥidun, "Unitarians," a name derived from their emphasis on the absolute oneness of God (*tawḥid*). They deny all acts implying polytheism, such as visiting tombs and venerating saints, and advocate a return to the original teachings of Islam as incorporated in the Qurʾān and Hadith (traditions of Muhammad), with condemnation of all innovations (*bidʿah*). Wahhābī theology and jurisprudence, based, respectively, on the teachings of Ibn Taymiyyah and on the legal school of Aḥmad ibn Ḥanbal, stress literal belief in the Qurʾan and Hadith and the establishment of a Muslim state based only on Islamic law.

SETTLEMENT PATTERNS

Qataris are largely urban dwellers; less than one-tenth of the population lives in rural areas. Doha, on the east coast, is Qatar's largest city and commercial centre and contains about half of the emirate's population. It has a deepwater port and an international airport. The main oil port and industrial centre is Umm Sa‘īd, to the south of Doha on the eastern coast. Al-Rayyān, just northwest of Doha, is the country's second major urban area. These three cities and many smaller settlements are linked by roads. Of the many islands and coral reefs belonging to Qatar, Ḥālūl, in the Persian Gulf 60 miles (97 km) east of Doha, serves as a collecting and storage point for the country's three offshore oil fields.

DEMOGRAPHIC TRENDS

The population of Qatar has been steadily growing; in spite of a markedly low death rate, however, a modest birth rate has led to a rate of natural increase that is slightly lower than the world average. Males outnumber females by more than three to one—in large part because of the disproportionate number of expatriate males. The average life expectancy is about 74 years for males and 76 years for females.

CHAPTER 17

The Qatari Economy

Qatar's economic prosperity is derived from the extraction and export of petroleum—discovered in 1939 and first produced in 1949—and natural gas. Before World War II, Qatar's population engaged in pearling, fishing, and some trade (with little exception the only occupations available) and was one of the poorest in the world. By the 1970s, however, native Qataris enjoyed one of the highest per capita incomes in the world, in spite of subsequent declines in income due to fluctuations in world oil prices. Qatar's original oil concession was granted to the Iraq Petroleum Company (IPC), a consortium of European and American firms. This and later concessions were nationalized in the 1970s. While state-owned Qatar Petroleum (formerly Qatar General Petroleum Corporation) oversees oil operations, private corporations continue to play an important role as service companies.

Agriculture and Fishing

The government has attempted to modernize the fishing and agriculture sectors by offering interest-free loans; yet food production continues to generate only a tiny fraction of the country's gross domestic product (GDP). The scarcity of fertile land and water imposes severe limitations on agriculture, and a large proportion of the country's food must be imported. Use of treated sewage effluent and desalinated water for irrigation, however, has helped to expand the production of fruits such as dates and melons and vegetables such as tomatoes, squash, and eggplant, which Qatar now exports to other Persian Gulf countries. Production of meat, cereal-grains, and milk also began to increase by the end of the 20th century.

Fishing and pearling—once the mainstays of Qatar's economy—have greatly declined in importance. Pearling is almost non-existent, in large part because of Japan's dominant cultured-pearl industry. The government maintains a fishing fleet and since the late 1990s has placed greater emphasis on commercial fishing and shrimp harvesting.

RESOURCES AND POWER

Qatar's petroleum reserves, found both onshore along the western coast at Dukhān and offshore from the eastern coast, are modest by regional standards. However, oil dominates Qatar's economy, accounting for much of government revenues and the country's GDP (although it employs only a small proportion of the country's workforce).

In an attempt to reduce its dependency on oil, Qatar began to develop its natural gas resources in the mid-1990s. The country possesses enormous deposits of natural gas,

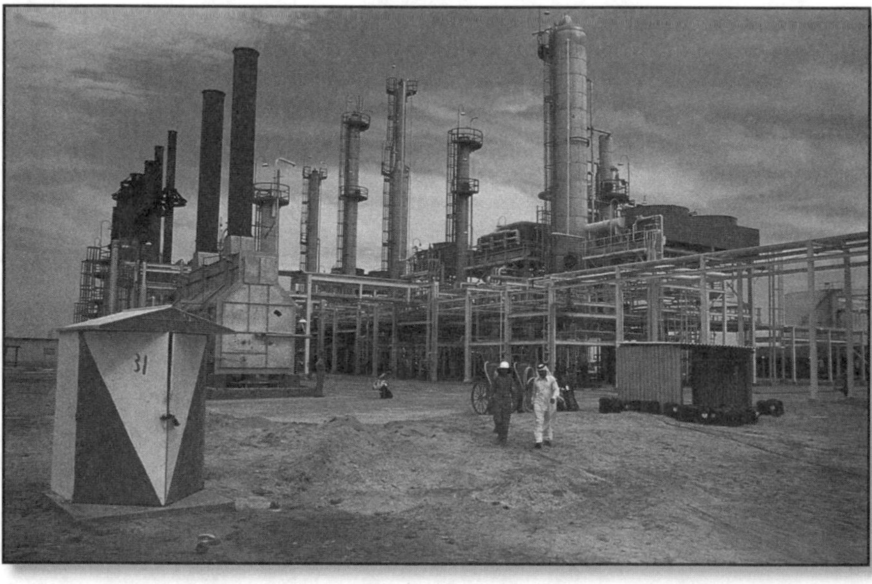

Oil refinery on the island of Hālūl, Qatar, in the Persian Gulf. © Peter Sanders

and its offshore North Field is one of the largest gas fields in the world. To develop its gas fields, Qatar had to borrow heavily, but high oil prices in the early 21st century put the country on more firm financial footing. Qatar's strategy has been to develop its natural gas reserves aggressively through joint projects with major international oil and gas companies, focusing on the North Field.

MANUFACTURING

Qatar has sought to diversify its economy through industrialization. Most of the manufacturing sector comprises large firms of mixed state and foreign private ownership. For example, the Qatar Petrochemical Company is largely owned by a government holding company, and a French firm has a minor stake. Flour milling and cement production have also been undertaken. Diversification by expanding manufacturing depends on an abundance of cheap energy for running plants, however, and is thus tied to Qatar's hydrocarbon resources. Its natural gas reserves have been used to develop a strong liquefied natural gas (LNG) industry.

FINANCE

Qatar has a relatively small banking system, which is one of the least developed of the Arab gulf states. The Qatar Central Bank, founded in 1993, provides banking functions for the state and issues the Qatari rial, the national currency. In addition to domestic banks, including commercial, development, and Islamic banks (institutions bound by strict religious rules governing transactions), licensed foreign banks are also authorized to operate. Qatar has been generous in its foreign aid disbursements, particularly to other Arab and Islamic countries. The Doha Stock Exchange began operations in 1997.

TRADE

Machinery and transport equipment, iron and steel, manufactured goods, and food and live animals are Qatar's major imports. Crude petroleum, LNG, and refined petroleum account for the bulk of the value of exports. Japan, South Korea, and the United Arab Emirates are among Qatar's most important trading partners—Japan receives by far the largest proportion of Qatar's exports, largely in the form of petroleum and petroleum products.

SERVICES

The service sector, including public administration and defense, accounts for some one-fourth of Qatar's GDP and employs more than half of the workforce. In an attempt to further diversify Qatar's economy, the government has sought to develop tourism, in particular by promoting the country as a site for international conferences; however, tourism remains a relatively small component of the economy.

LABOUR AND TAXATION

Foreigners account for the great bulk of Qatar's workforce, a matter of continuing concern for Qatari officials. Qatar has banned the employment of Egyptians since 1996, when the government claimed that Egypt was involved in an unsuccessful coup. The government has actively pursued programs to encourage employing and promoting Qatari nationals in the workforce. However, a five-year plan introduced in 2000 to boost significantly the number of Qataris in the labour force fell far short of its goals. Labour unions and associations are forbidden. The standard workweek is Sunday through Thursday.

Qatar does not levy taxes on personal income nor does it have sales or value-added taxes. Foreign corporations (excluding those owned by Gulf Cooperation Council members) are taxed, but the amount accounts for only a small proportion of the government's revenue; the bulk of its revenue comes from the sale of petroleum and natural gas.

TRANSPORTATION AND TELECOMMUNICATIONS

Qatar has an extensive road network, nearly all of which is paved. Although there are no railroads, a rail system is under development. The country has several important ports, including those at Doha and Umm Saʿīd. An international airport is located at Doha, and Qatar Airways is the country's national carrier.

Qatar Public Telecommunications Corporation (Q-Tel) is the sole provider of telecommunication services in the country. It also sets policies and makes administrative decisions for the sector. In 1996 the Internet was made available to the public, with Q-Tel as the sole service provider. Internet use is highest among Qatari nationals. A submarine fibre-optic cable system completed in the late 1990s links Qatar with Bahrain, Oman, and Kuwait.

CHAPTER 18

Qatari Government and Society

A constitutional emirate with one advisory body, Qatar is ruled by a hereditary emir from the Āl Thānī family. Members of the ruling family hold almost all the major ministerial posts, which are appointed by the emir. The family, however, is large and fragmented. As oil revenues rose after World War II, contention within the ruling family grew, and there have been several bloodless palace coups.

The emir's power is constrained by the need to maintain the support of important family members, many of whom occupy high governmental posts. The homogeneity of the ruling family and the country's wealth contribute to Qatar's political stability. The emir has also cautiously expanded political participation, allowing the first municipal elections to take place in 1999, with an electorate that included both female and male Qataris. Under a provisional constitution enacted in 1972, the emir ruled in consultation with a Council of Ministers (Majlis al-Wuzarā') and an appointed Advisory Council (Majlis al-Shūrā). However, a new constitution was approved by referendum in 2003 and enacted in 2005; among its provisions was a new National Assembly, two-thirds of whose members would be popularly elected and one-third appointed.

Justice

Qatar's legal system has several sources: the Sharīʿah (Islamic law), Ottoman law, and European civil and (to a lesser extent) common law. The latter was introduced through the borrowing of codes of other European-influenced Arab states. Personal status law is governed largely by the Sharīʿah, while criminal law is influenced but not governed by it. In addition to a Higher Judicial Council, there are also

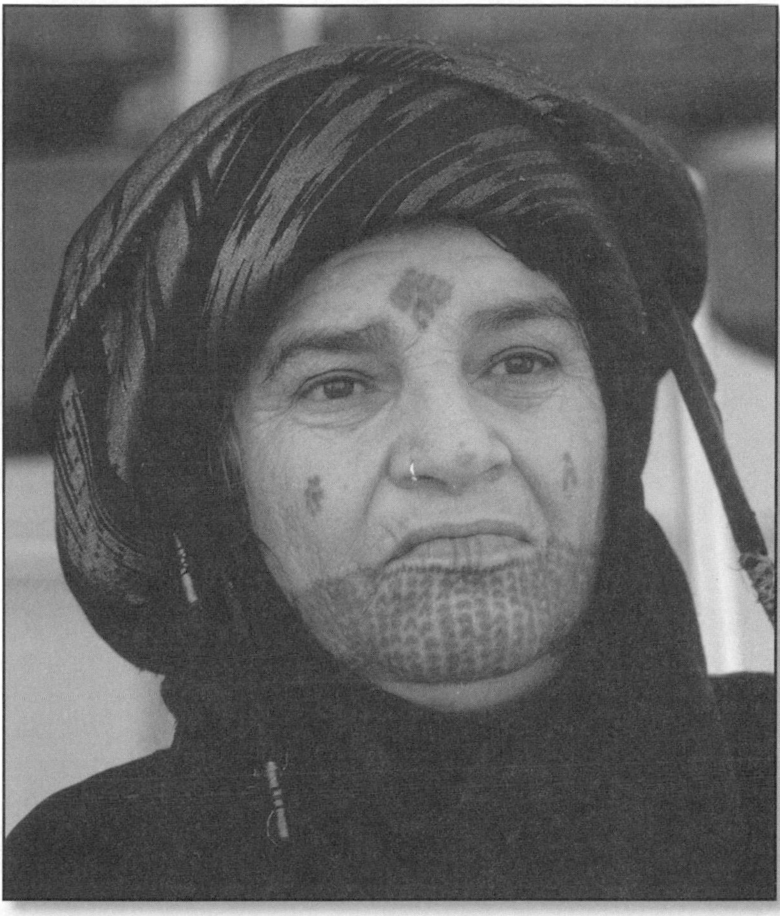

Woman with traditional tattooed markings on her face. Women have the right both to vote and run for office in Qatar. TG Stock/Tim Graham Photo Library/Getty Images

several lower courts and a system of appeals courts. The emir sometimes acts as the final court of appeal. Formal civil and criminal codes were introduced in the 1970s.

POLITICAL PROCESS

There are no political parties in Qatar. Since 1999, Qataris have been allowed to vote in municipal elections. Voting

Thānī Dynasty

The Thānī dynasty (Arabic: Āl Thānī, "Thānī family") is the ruling family of Qatar. The Āl Thānī are from the Tamīm tribe, which migrated eastward from central Arabia to the Qatar peninsula and emerged as a dominant ruling family in the mid-19th century. The second sheikh, Qāsim ibn Muḥammad (ruled 1878–1913), is considered Qatar's founder. The seventh sheikh, Khalīfah ibn Ḥamad (ruled 1972–95), was instrumental in obtaining Qatar's independence from Britain in 1971 and became the first emir. The clan is especially large among the ruling families of the gulf states.

is open to all citizens aged 18 years and older, except for members of the police and armed forces, and women are allowed to stand for public office.

SECURITY

Military service is voluntary for males aged 18 years and older. Qatar has a small defense force—of some 12,000 troops, most of whom serve in the army—and the country depends on the protection of its neighbours and allies to deter possible external threats. The country's military expenditure as a percentage of its GDP, however, is high: at five times the world average, it spends more than almost any other country.

HEALTH AND WELFARE

Health care and medical services are provided free to all residents through government programs. The government also funds recreational and cultural clubs and facilities for young people as part of its extensive "youth welfare" campaign.

EDUCATION

Education is free but not compulsory for all citizens between the ages of 6 and 16. Classes are segregated by sex. Qatar spends generously on education, having one of the highest per-pupil expenditures in the world. Its system has expanded rapidly. Two teacher-training faculties, one for men and one for women, were established in 1973, and together they were given university status, as the University of Qatar, in 1977. The university has continued to expand, and a new campus was completed in Doha in 1985. The Qatar Foundation for Education, Science, and Community Development (established 1995) works with international organizations to develop additional educational facilities.

Interest in establishing Qatar as a major regional research hub led to the foundation of Education City, a multi-university facility located on the outskirts of Doha. By the early 21st century several American institutions had branches in Education City, including Virginia Commonwealth University, Weill Cornell Medical College (part of Cornell University), Carnegie Mellon University, Texas A&M University, Northwestern University, and Georgetown University. The universities offered programs such as premedical and medical studies, business administration, chemical, electrical, and mechanical engineering, journalism, and fine arts.

The government also provides adult education classes in schools and centres throughout the country, with an emphasis on increasing adult literacy. About four-fifths of the country's population is literate, with roughly equal proportions of males and females.

CHAPTER 19

QATARI CULTURAL LIFE

The Qatari people are descendants of Bedouin and have maintained a tradition of generous hospitality. Qatari society is centred on Islamic customs and tends to be conservative in most respects. The consumption of alcohol, for example, is frowned upon, although alcohol may be served in a limited number of hotels catering mainly to foreigners. Likewise, dress is generally traditional and conservative. Qatari Arab men usually dress in a flowing white shirt (*thawb*) and a head scarf (*kaffiyeh*) held in place by a cord (*ʿiqāl*). Dress for Qatari women, although still conservative, is much less strict than in neighbouring Saudi Arabia. Many women still wear the full length black cloak (*ʿabāyah*), generally over Western clothing, but others simply wear the veil (*ḥijāb*). Their traditional dress is often decorated with gold or silver embroidery. In public the sexes are customarily separated.

Qatari cuisine features fresh fish and rice cooked with Indian spices. A typical meal might include broiled fish served on a bed of spiced rice with curry and potatoes. Coffee is the beverage of choice and is usually served strong, boiling hot, and without sugar. The capital of Doha also abounds in restaurants offering cuisines from throughout the world.

Qataris celebrate the standard Islamic holidays, including Ramadan and the two *ʿīd*s, ʿĪd al-Fiṭr and ʿĪd al-Aḍḥā. They also celebrate several secular holidays, such as Independence Day and the anniversary of the emir's ascension to power.

THE ARTS

The Qatari Fine Arts Society promotes and exhibits work by local painters, as do the galleries to be found in Doha.

ʿĪd al-Fiṭr

ʿĪd al-Fiṭr (Arabic: Festival of Breaking Fast), also called al-ʿĪd al-Ṣaghīr, is the first of two canonical festivals of Islam. ʿĪd al-Fiṭr marks the end of Ramadan, the Muslim holy month of fasting, and is celebrated during the first three days of Shawwal, the 10th month of the Islamic calendar (though the Muslim use of a lunar calendar means that it may fall in any season of the year). As in Islam's other holy festival, ʿĪd al-Aḍḥā, it is distinguished by the performance of communal prayer (*ṣalāt*) at daybreak on its first day. It is a time of official receptions and private visits, when friends greet one another, presents are given, new clothes are worn, and the graves of relatives are visited.

The National Council for Culture, Arts, and Heritage and several other agencies and departments oversee literary, artistic, and cultural activities as well as recreation and tourism. The traditional Bedouin arts of weaving (mostly rugs and pillows), poetry, and singing are still practiced. A genre of music known as *nahmah*, once popular among pearl divers in Qatar and the broader Persian Gulf region, virtually disappeared with the decline of the pearling industry, although the Qatari government has made great efforts to preserve it. Arab, Pakistani, Indian, and other expatriate workers have brought their musical styles to the country, but Qatari youth listen more to Western and Arab popular music than to Bedouin or other traditional forms.

CULTURAL INSTITUTIONS

Located in a former palace, the Qatar National Museum (founded 1975), in Doha, includes displays on the country's history and archaeology as well as a model lagoon in which Qatari sailing and pearling vessels are featured; the museum's large aquarium is a popular attraction. A fort at Doha has been converted into a museum for traditional crafts. Qatar's National Theatre performs programs in the capital.

SPORTS AND RECREATION

Qatar's sports culture blends the traditional sports of Arabia's desert society with contemporary sports of Western origin. Popular traditional sports include Arabian horse racing, camel racing, and falconry, all rooted in the country's nomadic past. Western sports such as basketball, golf, handball, football (soccer), swimming, table tennis, track, and volleyball are practiced widely, but primarily by the expatriate population; football is overwhelmingly the most popular of these. The country also hosts several annual sporting events, of which tennis, golf, and automobile racing are the most notable. The Qatar National Sport Federation, founded in 1961, serves as an organizing body for sports education. Qatar made its Olympic debut at the 1984 Summer Games.

MEDIA AND PUBLISHING

Government-owned radio and television stations broadcast in Arabic, English, French, and Urdu. Satellite television transmissions from outside the country are easily accessible through local providers, and Qatar receives radio broadcasts from the neighbouring gulf states and international broadcasters. In 1996 media restrictions in Qatar were relaxed—the country's press is among the freest in the region—and that year al-Jazeera, a satellite

Journalists working in the newsroom at the headquarters of the Qatar based al-Jazeera satellite news channel in Doha on November 14, 2006. Karim Jaafar/AFP/Getty Images

television network, was founded by a member of the ruling family. The outspoken news channel is received throughout much of the Muslim world and has become one of the most popular stations in the Middle East, as well as one of the most important sources of news in a region where there is little toleration for a free press. It became internationally known in 2001 after broadcasting several speeches and interviews of the militant Islamist Osama bin Laden. Several local daily newspapers and weekly publications are also available in Qatar.

CHAPTER 20

Qatar: Past and Present

Little is known of Qatar's history before the 18th century, when the region's population consisted largely of Bedouin nomads and there were only a few small fishing villages. Qatar's modern history conventionally begins in 1766 with the migration to the peninsula of families from Kuwait, notably the Āl Khalīfah. Their settlement at the new town of Al-Zubārah grew into a small pearl-diving and trade centre. In 1783 the Āl Khalīfah led the conquest of nearby Bahrain, where they remained the ruling family into the 21st century. Following the departure of the Āl Khalīfah from Qatar, the country was ruled by a series of transitory sheikhs, the most famous of whom was Raḥmah ibn Jābir al-Jalāhimah, who was regarded by the British as a leading pirate of the so-called Pirate Coast.

Qatar came to the attention of the British in 1867 when a dispute between the Bahraini Āl Khalīfah, who continued to hold some claim to Al-Zubārah, and the Qatari residents escalated into a major confrontation, in the course of which Doha was virtually destroyed. Until the attack, Britain had viewed Qatar as a Bahraini dependency. It then signed a separate treaty with Muḥammad ibn Thānī in 1868, setting the course both for Qatar's future independence and for the rule of the Āl Thānī, who until the treaty were only one among several important families on the peninsula.

Ottoman forces, which had conquered the nearby Al-Hasa province of Saudi Arabia, occupied Qatar in 1871 at the invitation of the ruler's son, then left following the Saudi reconquest of Al-Hasa in 1913. In 1916 Britain signed a treaty with Qatar's leader that resembled earlier agreements with other gulf states, giving Britain control over foreign policy in return for British protection.

In 1935 Qatar signed a concession agreement with the Iraq Petroleum Company; four years later oil was discovered. Oil was not recovered on a commercial scale, however, until 1949. The revenues from the oil company, later named Petroleum Development (Qatar) Limited and then the Qatar Petroleum Company, rose dramatically. The distribution of these revenues stirred serious infighting in the Āl Thānī, prompting the British to intervene in the succession of 1949 and eventually precipitating a palace coup in 1972 that brought Sheikh Khalīfah ibn Ḥamad Āl Thānī to power. In 1968 Britain announced plans to withdraw from the gulf. After negotiations with neighbouring sheikhdoms—those comprising the present United Arab Emirates and Bahrain—Qatar declared independence on Sept. 1, 1971. The earlier agreements with Britain were replaced with a treaty of friendship. That same month, Qatar became a member of the Arab League and of the UN. In 1981 the emirate joined its five Arab gulf neighbours in establishing the Gulf Cooperation Council, an alliance formed to promote economic cooperation and enhance both internal security and external defense against the threats generated by the Islamic revolution in Iran and the Iran-Iraq War.

Qatari troops participated in the Persian Gulf War of 1990–91, notably in the battle for control of the Saudi border town of Ra's al-Khafjī on January 30–31. Doha, which served as a base for offensive strikes by French, Canadian, and U.S. aircraft against Iraq and the Iraqi forces occupying Kuwait, remained minimally affected by the conflict.

Renewed arguments over the distribution of oil revenues also caused the 1995 palace coup that brought Sheikh Khalīfah's son, Sheikh Ḥamad, to power. Although his father had permitted Ḥamad to take over day-to-day governing some years before, Khalīfah contested the coup. Before Ḥamad fully consolidated his power, he had

Qatari women walk through the streets of Souk Waqif, a market in Doha, on March 14, 2010. Valery Hache/AFP/Getty Images

to weather an attempted countercoup in 1996 and a protracted lawsuit with his father over the rightful ownership of billions of dollars of invested oil revenues, which was finally settled out of court.

During the 1990s Qatar agreed to permit U.S. military forces to place equipment in several sites throughout the country and granted them use of Qatari airstrips during U.S. operations in Afghanistan in 2001. These agreements were formalized in late 2002, and Qatar became the headquarters for American and allied military operations in Iraq the following year.

CHAPTER 21

United Arab Emirates: The Land and Its People

The United Arab Emirates is a federation of seven emirates along the eastern coast of the Arabian Peninsula. The largest of these emirates, Abu Dhabi (Abu Zaby), which comprises more than three-fourths of the federation's total land area, is the centre of its oil industry and borders Saudi Arabia on the federation's southern and eastern borders. The port city of Dubai, located at the base of the mountainous Musandam Peninsula, is the capital of the emirate of Dubai (Dubayy) and is one of the region's most vital commercial and financial centres, housing hundreds of multinational corporations in a forest of skyscrapers. The smaller emirates of Al-Shāriqah (Sharjah), ʿAjmān, Umm al-Qaywayn, and Ra's al-Khayman also occupy the peninsula, whose protrusion north toward Iran forms the Strait of Hormuz linking the Persian Gulf to the Gulf of Oman. The federation's seventh member, Al-Fujayrah, faces the Gulf of Oman and is the only member of the union with no frontage along the Persian Gulf.

The United Arab Emirates, which is slightly smaller in area than Portugal, is bordered by Qatar to the northwest, Saudi Arabia to the west and south, and Oman to the east and northeast. Since the early 1990s the emirates have been in a dispute with Iran over the ownership of three islands: Abū Mūsā and Greater and Lesser Tunb (Ṭunb al-Kubrā and Ṭunb al-Ṣughrā). In addition, the border with Saudi Arabia has never been defined, which was not an issue until Saudi Arabia began production at the Shaybah oil field in the border region in 1998.

Citizens of the United Arab Emirates are a minority; they account for only about one-fifth of the country's population. The majority of the population is made up of foreign workers, many of whom are from other Arab countries or from South Asia.

RELIEF

Nearly the entire country is desert, containing broad areas of sand. Some of the world's largest sand dunes are located east of 'Arādah in the oases of Al-Liwā'. Important oases are at Al-'Ayn about 100 miles (160 km) east of Abu Dhabi. Along the eastern portion of the Musandam Peninsula, the northern extension of the Ḥajar Mountains (also shared by Oman) offers the only other major relief feature; elevations rise to about 6,500 feet (2,000 m) at their highest point. The Persian Gulf coast is broken by shoals and dotted with islands that offer shelter to small vessels. There are, however, no natural deepwater harbours; both Dubai's Port Rāshid and the massive Port Jabal 'Alī, 20 miles (32 km) southwest of Dubai city, are man-made, as are major ports in the emirates of Abu Dhabi, Al-Shāriqah, and Ra's al-Khaymah. The coast of the Gulf of Oman is more regular and has three natural harbours—Dibā, Khawr Fakkān, and Kalbā.

DRAINAGE

The United Arab Emirates has no perennial streams nor any regularly occurring bodies of surface water. Precipitation, what little falls, is drained from the mountains in the form of seasonal wadis that terminate in inland salt flats, or *sabkhah*s, whose drainage is frequently blocked by the country's constantly shifting dunes. In the far west the Maṭṭī Salt Flat extends southward into Saudi Arabia, and coastal *sabkhah*s, which are occasionally inundated by the waters of the Persian Gulf, lie in the areas around Abu Dhabi.

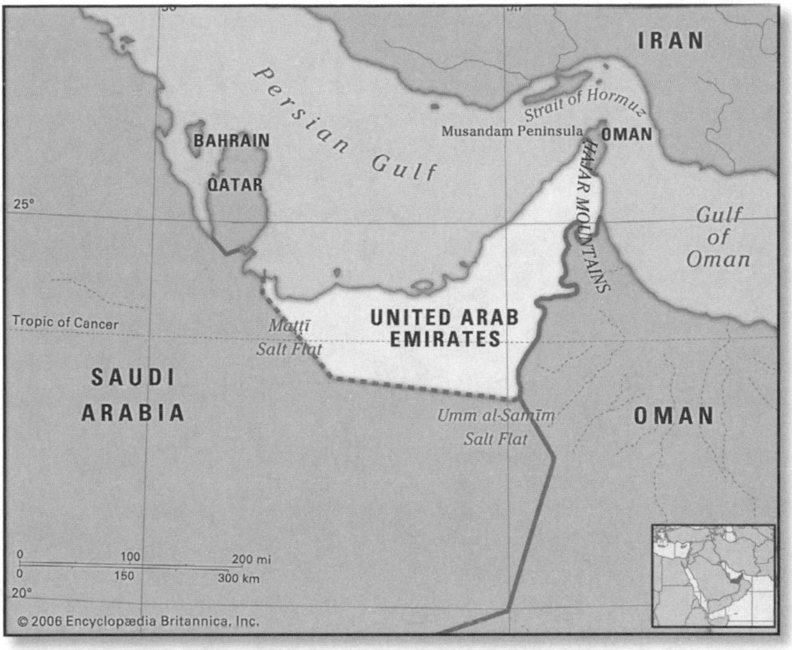

CLIMATE

The climate is hot and humid along the coast and is hotter still, but dry, in the interior. Precipitation averages only 4 to 6 inches (100 to 150 mm) annually, though it fluctuates considerably from year to year. January temperatures average in the mid-60s F (high 10s C), while in July the temperature averages in the low 90s F (low 30s C). Summertime highs can reach 115 °F (46 °C) on the coast and 120 °F (49 °C) or more in the desert. In midwinter and early summer, winds known as the *shamāl* (Arabic: "norther") blow from the north and northwest, bearing dust and sand.

PLANT AND ANIMAL LIFE

Because of the desert climate, vegetation is scanty and largely limited to the low shrubs that offer forage to

Musandam Peninsula

The Musandam Peninsula is a northeastern extension of the Arabian Peninsula, separating the Gulf of Oman on the east from the Persian Gulf on the west to form the Strait of Hormuz to the north. The Ru'ūs al-Jibāl ("the Mountaintops"), the northernmost extremity of the Western Ḥajar mountains, occupy the northern tip of the Musandam Peninsula; this area is a part of Oman, and is separated from the rest of the country (to the south) by the United Arab Emirates. The peninsula is generally about 22 miles (35 km) wide. Al-Shamm Channel (also called Elphinstone Inlet) and Al-Ghazīrah Bay (Malcom Inlet) deeply incise the coastline from west and east a few miles south of the Strait of Hormuz and come within several hundred yards of bisecting the peninsula. Al-Shamm Channel is about 10 miles (16 km) long and is bordered by cliffs that rise to heights of 3,000 to 4,000 feet (900 to 1,200 m). The highest elevation on the mountainous peninsula is 6,847 feet (2,087 m) at Mount Al-Ḥartīm. The mountains slope steeply seaward forming an extremely rugged and rocky coast that makes Musandam a hazard to navigation. Wadi beds, where sporadic rains have carved deep ravines, are fertile with vegetation and the lower mountain slopes are covered with wild olive trees; juniper trees grow at the summits. Dates and vegetables are the main crops on the peninsula.

The peninsula is mainly inhabited by the Shiḥūḥ, who are fishermen and herdsmen and are probably descended from the original inhabitants of northern Oman, pushed into the mountains by successive Muslim and Portuguese invasions. Fishing is the peninsula's main industry with packing plants at Al-Khaṣab and Bay'ah. There are reserves of petroleum off the western coast of the Musandam Peninsula. Communication is mostly by sea, since no roads cross the forbidding terrain. The Sultanate of Oman has created the Musandam Development Committee for building fishing jetties, construction of the Khaṣab dam and food storage, and undertaking the Bay'ah power expansion project during the Second Development Plan (1981–85). The main population centre is the oasis town of Dibā on the peninsula's southeastern coast.

nomadic herds; but millions of trees, notably mangroves, have been planted in Abu Dhabi and have provided habitats for various species. In the oases, date palms are raised together with alfalfa (lucerne). Fruits are grown, and the Al-'Ayn oases east of Abu Dhabi are known for their mangoes. Animal life includes domesticated goats, sheep, and camels, together with cattle and poultry, which were introduced in more recent times. Wildlife consists of predators such as caracals, sand cats (*Felis margarita*), and the Ruppell's (*Vulpes ruppelli*) and red foxes; larger animals such as Arabian oryx and Arabian and Persian gazelles; smaller mammals such as cape hares, lesser jerboas, and various types of gerbils; and a variety of snakes and lizards. The gulf waters harbour schools of mackerel, grouper, tuna, and porgies, as well as sharks and occasional whales. In the 1990s the government initiated a conservation and management program to preserve and protect desert animal and plant life.

ETHNIC GROUPS

As mentioned before, only about one-fifth of the emirates' residents are citizens. The remainder are mostly foreign workers and their dependents, with South Asians constituting the largest of these groups. Arabs from countries other than the United Arab Emirates and Iranians account for another significant portion. Southeast Asians, including many Filipinos, have immigrated in increasing numbers to work in various capacities.

LANGUAGES AND RELIGION

The official language of the United Arab Emirates is Arabic. Modern Standard Arabic is taught in schools, and most native Emiratis speak a dialect of Gulf Arabic that is

Arabian oryx (Oryx leucoryx). Rod Moon—The National Audubon Society Collection/Photo Researchers

generally similar to that spoken in surrounding countries. A number of languages are spoken among the expatriate community, including various dialects of Pashto, Hindi, Balochi, and Persian. English is also widely spoken.

About three-fourths of the population is Muslim, of which roughly four-fifths belong to the Sunni branch of Islam; Shīʿite minorities can be found in Dubai and

Al-ʿAyn

Al-ʿAyn is a city in Al-Buraymī oasis, southeastern Abu Dhabi emirate, United Arab Emirates. The oasis city consists of houses of dried earth in a large palm grove; it also has a modern mosque and many gardens. Al-ʿAyn is situated in a large expanse of fertile land at the foot of Mount Ḥafīt. Grave mounds at Al-ʿAyn have tombs with figures of animals and people carved from stone and dating to about 2700 BCE. Across the desert from the oasis city stands a fortress known as the Eastern Fort, erected by Sheikh Sulṭān ibn Zāyid in 1910; it is one of several forts constructed by the Āl Nahyān in Al-ʿAyn. In 1952 the Saudis occupied a neighbouring village in Al-Buraymī oasis. Al-ʿAyn was assigned to Abu Dhabi emirate under an agreement with Oman in 1953. The Saudis withdrew their small force from Al-Buraymī oasis in 1955 after being defeated by the forces of the Sultan of Abu Dhabi, and the dispute was settled by an agreement signed in 1974.

Agriculture is the traditional economic activity; fodder and market garden crops are produced. An experimental farm (1967) at Al-ʿAyn concentrates on intensive stock raising, and significant portions of land have been reclaimed from the desert. Commercial poultry farming is also economically important. A network of roads radiates from Al-ʿAyn, connecting it with Abu Dhabi, the national capital. The city also has an airport. There are a number of industries, including a cement factory, a cable and electric-wire plant, a sheet-metal plant, a glass and ceramic factory, a flour mill, and a brickworks. A university was founded at Al-ʿAyn in 1976; a number of museums, including the Al-ʿAyn Palace Museum and Al-ʿAyn National Museum, are also located there.

Al-Shāriqah. There are also small but growing numbers of Christians and Hindus in the country.

SETTLEMENT PATTERNS AND DEMOGRAPHIC TRENDS

The population of the United Arab Emirates is concentrated primarily in cities along both coasts, although the interior oasis settlement of Al-ʿAyn has grown into a major population centre as well. Several emirates have exclaves within other emirates.

The federation's birth rate, well below the world average, is one of the lowest among the Persian Gulf states, and the infant mortality rate has decreased substantially. Owing to the large number of foreign workers, more than two-thirds of the population is male. The country's death rate is among the world's lowest, and the average life expectancy is about 73 years for men and 78 years for women. The major causes of death are cardiovascular disease, accidents, and cancer.

CHAPTER 22

The Emirati Economy

The federation's economy is dominated by the petroleum produced in the Abu Dhabi and Dubai emirates. The wealthiest of the emirates, Abu Dhabi contains nearly one-tenth of the world's proven oil reserves and contributes more than half of the national budget.

AGRICULTURE AND FISHING

Agricultural production—centred largely in the emirates of Ra's al-Khaymah and Al-Fujayrah, in the two exclaves of ʿAjmān, and at Al-ʿAyn—has expanded considerably through the increased use of wells and pumps to provide water for irrigation. However, agriculture contributes only a small fraction of the country's gross domestic product (GDP) and employs less than one-tenth of the workforce. Dates are a major crop, as are tomatoes, cucumbers, and eggplants, and the United Arab Emirates is nearly self-sufficient in fruit and vegetable production. The country also produces enough eggs, poultry, fish, and dairy products to meet its own needs but must import most other foodstuffs, notably grains. The Arid Lands Research Centre at Al-ʿAyn experiments with raising crops in a desert environment. Most commercial fishing is concentrated in Umm al-Qaywayn, and the emirates have one of the largest fishing sectors in the Arab world.

RESOURCES AND POWER

Oil was discovered in Abu Dhabi in 1958, and the government of that emirate owns a controlling interest in all oil-producing companies in the federation through the Abu Dhabi National Oil Company (ADNOC). Petroleum and natural gas production contributes more than one-third of GDP but employs only a tiny fraction of the workforce. The largest petroleum concessions are held by an ADNOC subsidiary, Abu Dhabi Marine Operating Company (ADMA-OPCO), which is partially owned by British, French, and Japanese interests. One of the main offshore fields is located in Umm al-Shā'if. Al-Bunduq offshore field is shared with neighbouring Qatar but is operated by ADMA-OPCO. A Japanese consortium operates an offshore rig at Al-Mubarraz, and other offshore concessions are held by American companies. Onshore oil concessions are held by another ADNOC company, the Abu Dhabi Company for Onshore Oil Operations, which is likewise partially owned by American, French, Japanese, and British interests. Other concessions also are held by Japanese companies.

Petroleum production in Dubai began in 1969. There are offshore oil fields at Ḥaql Fatḥ, Fallah, and Rāshid. Dubai owns a controlling interest in all oil produced in the emirate. Al-Shāriqah began producing oil in 1974; another field, predominantly yielding natural gas, was discovered six years later. In 1984 oil production began off the shore of Ra's al-Khaymah, in the Persian Gulf. Dubai produces about one-third of the country's total output of petroleum.

The federation's natural gas reserves are among the world's largest, and most fields are found in Abu Dhabi. In the late 1990s the United Arab Emirates began investing heavily to develop its natural gas sector, both for export and to fire domestic thermal power plants; at the beginning of the 21st century, however, crude petroleum exports continued to far outstrip exports of natural gas.

MANUFACTURING

The emirates have attempted to diversify their economy to avoid complete dependence on oil, and manufacturing has played a significant part in that effort. A petrochemical industrial complex has been established at Al-Ruways, 140 miles (225 km) southwest of Abu Dhabi city, with a petroleum refinery, a gas fractionation plant, and an ammonia and urea plant. Dubai's revenues have been invested in projects such as a dry dock and a trade centre; expansion of its airport began in 2002, and additional hotels have been built, including the striking Burj al-'Arab ("Tower of the Arabs"), which opened in the late 1990s. The city's Burj Khalifa ("Khalifa Tower," previously known as Burj Dubai), inaugurated in January 2010, easily broke the records for the world's tallest building and the tallest freestanding structure. Al-Shāriqah has built a cement plant, a plastic-pipe factory, and paint factories. Manufacturing accounts for about one-eighth of the country's GDP and employs a comparable proportion of the workforce.

FINANCE

The Central Bank of the United Arab Emirates was established in 1980, with Dubai and Abu Dhabi each depositing half of their revenues in the institution. The bank also issues the UAE dirham, the emirates' national currency. There are commercial, investment, development, foreign, and domestic banks as well as a bankers' association. In 1991 the worldwide operations of Abu Dhabi's Bank of Credit and Commerce International (BCCI), partly owned by the ruling family, were closed down after corrupt practices were uncovered, and the emirate subsequently created the

Burj Khalifa

The Burj Khalifa is a mixed-use skyscraper in Dubai, U.A.E., that is the world's tallest building, according to all three of the main criteria by which such buildings are judged. Burj Khalifa ("Khalifa Tower"), known during construction as Burj Dubai, was officially named to honour the president of the neighbouring emirate of Abu Dhabi, Sheikh Khalīfah ibn Zāyid Āl Nahyān. Although the tower was formally opened on Jan. 4, 2010, the entirety of the interior was not complete at that time. Built to house a variety of commercial, residential, and hospitality ventures, the tower—whose intended height remained a closely guarded secret throughout its construction—reached completion at 162 floors and a height of 2,717 feet (828 m). It was designed by the Chicago-based architectural firm of Skidmore, Owings & Merrill. Adrian Smith served as architect, and William F. Baker served as structural engineer.

The building, modular in plan, is laid out on a three-lobed footprint that is an abstract rendering of the local *Hymenocallis* flower. The Y-shaped plan plays a central role in the reduction of wind forces on the tower. A hexagonal central core is buttressed by a series of wings, each with its own concrete core and perimeter columns. As the tower increases in height, the wings step back in a spiral configuration, changing the building's shape at each tier and so reducing the effect of the wind on the building. The central core emerges at the tower's top and is finished with a spire, which reaches more than 700 feet (200 m). The spire was constructed inside the tower and hoisted to its final position using a hydraulic pump. At the foundational level, the tower is supported by a reinforced concrete mat nearly 13 feet (4 m) thick, itself supported by concrete piles 5 feet (1.5 m) in diameter. A three-story podium anchors the tower in place; the podium and two-story basement alone measure some 2,000,000 square feet (186,000 square m) in their own right. The tower's exterior cladding is made up of aluminum and stainless-steel panels, vertical stainless-steel tubular fins, and more than 28,000 hand-cut glass panels. A public observation deck, called "At the Top," is located on the 124th floor.

Upon its inauguration in January 2010, Burj Khalifa easily surpassed the Taipei 101 (Taipei Financial Center) building in Taipei,

Taiwan, which measured 1,667 feet (508 m), as the world's tallest building. At the same time, Burj Khalifa broke numerous other records, including the world's tallest freestanding structure, the world's highest occupied floor, and the world's highest outdoor observation deck.

The opening ceremony for the Burj Khalifa building in Dubai, United Arab Emirates, on Monday, Jan. 4, 2010. Bloomberg via Getty Images

Abu Dhabi Free Zone Authority to develop a new financial centre. The emirates' first official stock exchange, the Dubai Financial Market (Sūq Dubayy al-Mālī), was opened in 2000, followed by the Dubai International Financial Exchange in 2005.

Finance is an important component of the emirates' economy, and the country's liberal banking regulations have made it a popular destination for foreign funds, both open and clandestine. Dubai in particular has become a major world banking centre and a hub for unofficial financial institutions known as *ḥawālah*s (or *hundī*s), which specialize in transferring money internationally beyond state regulation. While such institutions are used primarily to transfer remittances, they also have been a way for terrorist organizations and criminal groups to move and launder illicit funds.

TRADE

Trade has long been important to Dubai and Al-Shāriqah. Even before the discovery of oil, Dubai's prosperity was assured by its role as the Persian Gulf's leading entrepôt. (It was known especially as a route for smuggling gold into India.) In 1995 the United Arab Emirates joined the World Trade Organization and since then has developed a number of free-trade zones, technology parks, and modern ports in order to attract trade. The large free-trade zone of Port Jabal ʿAlī was developed during the 1980s and has done much to attract foreign manufacturing industries interested in producing goods for export.

Exports are dominated by petroleum and natural gas. Imports consist primarily of machinery and transport equipment, gold, precious stones and foods. Major trading partners include Japan, western European countries,

South Korea, and China. A large amount of trade is in reexports to neighbouring gulf countries.

SERVICES

The service sector, including public administration, defense, tourism, and construction, employs roughly two-fifths of the workforce and accounts for some one-fifth of GDP. Tourism has played an increasing role in the economy since the late 1990s. In order to develop its tourism sector, the government has encouraged hotel, resort, and restaurant construction and airport expansion.

LABOUR AND TAXATION

Expatriate workers constitute about nine-tenths of the labour force, and more in some private sector areas. Conditions for these workers often can be harsh, and at the beginning of the 21st century, the state did not allow workers to organize. Like other gulf states that depend heavily on foreign workers, the emirates have attempted to reduce the number of foreign employees—in a program known as Emiratization—by providing incentives for businesses to hire Emirati nationals. There are no personal taxes in the United Arab Emirates, and corporate taxes are levied only on oil companies and foreign banks. The bulk of government revenue is generated from nontax incomes, largely from the sale of petroleum products. In the early 21st century the expatriate labour issue persisted in spite of landmark developments. New laws were instituted that ban work during the heat of the midday hours in summer and that prohibit the use of children (largely expatriate) as jockeys in camel races. In addition, a number of strikes and protests in 2005 by unpaid expatriate labourers against a major construction and development company were resolved in favour of the workers. Early in 2006, the government announced the drafting of a new law permitting the formation of unions and wage bargaining; later that year, however, it instead passed a law permitting the deportation of striking workers, and worker organization remained illegal.

TRANSPORTATION AND TELECOMMUNICATIONS

An excellent road system, developed in the late 1960s and '70s, carries motor vehicles throughout the country and links it to its neighbours. The addition of a tunnel to the bridges connecting Dubai city and the nearby commercial centre of Dayrah facilitates the movement of traffic across the small saltwater inlet that separates them. The cities of Abu Dhabi, Dubai, Sharjah, Ra's al-Khaymah, and Al-Fujayrah are served by international airports; a sixth airport at Al-'Ayn was completed in the mid-1990s. The airport at Dubai is one of the busiest in the Middle East. The federation has a number of large and modern seaports, including the facilities at Dubai's Port Rāshid, which is serviced by a vast shipyard, and Port Jabal 'Alī, situated in one of the largest man-made harbours in the world and one of the busiest ports in the gulf. Of the smaller harbours on the Gulf of Oman, Al-Shāriqah has a modest port north of the city. In September 2009 the first portion of a remote-controlled rapid-transit metro line—the gulf region's first metro system—began operations in Dubai. Additional public transit projects, including monorail service in Abu Dhabi and linkages to the Saudi rail networks, were under consideration.

The state-controlled Emirates Telecommunications Corporation, known as Etisalat (Ittiṣālāt), is a major telecommunications provider in the country. Radio, television, telephone, and cellular telephone service is prevalent and widely used. In 2000 Etisalat began providing Internet service, and the emirates soon had one of the largest subscriber bases per capita in the Middle East. In 2005 a second licensed operator, Emirates Integrated Telecommunications Company (du), began providing telephone and high-speed Internet service, and in 2006 they reached an agreement with Etisalat to link their networks.

CHAPTER 23

Emirati Government and Society

The highest governmental authority is the Supreme Council of Rulers, which is composed of the quasi-hereditary rulers of the seven emirates. The president and vice president of the federation are elected for five-year terms by the Supreme Council from among its members. The president appoints a prime minister and a cabinet. The unicameral legislature, the Federal National Council, is an advisory body made up of 40 members appointed by the individual emirates for two-year terms. A provisional constitution was ratified in 1971 and was made permanent in 1996 by the Supreme Council.

LOCAL GOVERNMENT

The United Arab Emirates has a federal system of government, and any powers not assigned to the federal government by the constitution devolve to the constituent emirates. Generally, the distribution of power within the federal system is similar to those in other such systems—for example, the federation government administers foreign policy, determines broad economic policy, and runs the social welfare system—and a significant amount of power is exercised at the individual emirate level, notably in Abu Dhabi and Dubai.

JUSTICE

The constitution calls for a legal code based on Sharīʿah (Islamic law). In practice, the judiciary blends Western and Islamic legal principles. At the federal level the judicial branch consists of the Union Supreme Court and several courts of first instance: the former deals with emirate-federal or inter-emirate disputes and crimes against the state, and the latter cover administrative, commercial, and civil disputes between individuals and the federal government. Other legal matters are left to local judicial bodies.

POLITICAL PROCESS

Until the beginning of the 21st century, there were no political parties in the emirates, and no elections were held. In late 2006 a limited number of participants were permitted to vote in the first-ever elections. An electoral college of about 7,000 (less than 1 percent of the population) was eligible to participate in the selection of half of the membership of the advisory Federal National Council; the other half was to remain designated by appointment. On the whole, leadership in each emirate falls to that emirate's most politically prominent tribe (an agnatic lineage group composed of a number of related families), and the paramount leader, the emir, is selected by the notables of the ruling tribe from among their number—this is usually, but not always, a son of the previous emir. Each tribe, however, has its own leader, or sheikh, and a certain degree of political pluralism is necessary to maintain the ruling family's position. This is largely facilitated by the institution called the *majlis*, the council meeting. During the *majlis* the leader hears grievances, mediates disputes, and disperses largesse, and, in theory, anyone under the leader's rule must be granted access to the *majlis*.

SECURITY

The emirates' defense forces were merged in 1976, but the forces in Dubai and Abu Dhabi have retained some independence. The Supreme Council has made the right to raise armed forces a power of the national government. In 2006 the Supreme National Security Council, which included the president, prime minister, and chief of staff of the armed forces, among others, was formed to deal with the emirates' security needs. The number of uniformed military personnel is high for a country the size of the emirates, as is total military spending per capita. Most personnel are in the army, but the emirates maintain a small navy and air force, and a large number of expatriates serve in the military.

HEALTH AND WELFARE

Hospital services are free to nationals, and medical services are concentrated in Dubai and Abu Dhabi, which have numerous hospitals, child-welfare clinics, and other health facilities. In the late 1990s the emirates began privatizing health care, which led to a significant rise in the number of hospitals and physicians. Government spending on health care has also increased.

HOUSING

A considerable proportion of government spending, at both the federal and local levels, is devoted to constructing and financing housing and to developing civil infrastructure such as power, water, and waste removal. The federation government makes housing available to citizens through direct low-interest loans, subsidies on rental units, and grants of housing at no charge, and thousands of Emiratis have taken advantage of these programs.

EDUCATION

Education in the emirates is free and mandatory at the primary level for all children from ages 6 to 12. Secondary

Students line up as they enter their classroom on the first day of the academic year for public schools in Dubai on September 27, 2009. Karim Sahib/AFP/ Getty Images

education is not compulsory. There are a number of fine institutions of higher education in the emirates, and both boys and girls attend public school. Female students far outnumber males at the United Arab Emirates University, which opened at Al-'Ayn in 1977, and Zayed University (1998) provides women with technical education. At the beginning of the 21st century, more than three-fourths of the population was literate, and the female literacy rate exceeded that for men.

CHAPTER 24

Emirati Cultural Life

The cultural traditions of the United Arab Emirates are rooted in Islam and resonate with the wider Arab world, especially with the neighbouring states of the Persian Gulf. The federation has experienced the impact of Islamic resurgence, though Islam in the emirates is generally less austere than in Saudi Arabia. Tribal identities in the United Arab Emirates remain fairly strong, in spite of urbanization and the presence of a large expatriate community, and the family is still considered the strongest and most cohesive social unit.

DAILY LIFE AND SOCIAL CUSTOMS

In several ways, change is apparent in the federation's cultural life. Changes in attitudes toward marriage and the employment of women are discernible. Some women are now given more choice in a marriage partner, and they have gained greater access to education and some types of professional work. New forms of entertainment, ranging from football (soccer) matches to DVD players, have affected taste and behaviour.

Although few Emiratis retain the lifeways of their forebears—practicing a nomadic lifestyle or plying the Persian Gulf in search of fish and pearls—many traditional modes of living continue. The major Islamic holidays, including the two *ʿīd*s (festivals), ʿĪd al-Fiṭr and ʿĪd al-Aḍḥā, are observed among the Muslim majority, and traditional dress is still the norm. For women, traditional attire consists of a light chemise known as a *dirʿ*, which is often worn beneath a more ornate dress (*thawb*). Beneath the dress a *sirwāl*, a type of loose trouser, is worn. Outside the home

The Mall of the Emirates, a huge shopping complex, in Dubai, United Arab Emirates, December 3, 2009. Dan Kitwood/Getty Images

or in the presence of strangers, women still cover themselves with a dark cloak known as an *ʿabāyah* and cover their heads with a scarf called a *shāl*, which may also serve as a veil (*ḥijāb* or *burquʿ*). Fabrics are often delicate, colourful, and highly embroidered, and Emirati women wear a variety of fine gold and silver jewelry.

The traditional garb for men consists of a long, simple, ankle-length garment known as a *dishdashah* (or *thawb*). Usually made of white cotton, the *dishdashah* may also be of a heavier material and may be made in a variety of colours. The standard head covering is the *ghuṭrah*, a light scarf (usually white or white and red checkered, also known as a kaffiyeh) held in place by a black cord of camel hair known as an *ʿiqāl*. Colour, style, and material of head-wear may vary among groups.

Camel Racing

Camel racing is the sport of running camels at speed, with a rider astride, over a predetermined course. The sport is generally limited to running the dromedary—whose name is derived from the Greek verb *dramein*, "to run"—rather than the Bactrian camel.

Camels are customarily used as a means of transportation and are reared for their meat, milk, and hides. Camel racing is, nonetheless, as old as history itself. On the Arabian Peninsula, the native habitat of the dromedary, it can be traced to at least the early Islamic period, in the 7th century CE. Although traditionally overshadowed by horse racing in that region—the peninsula is home to the Arabian horse—the racing of camels was long a folk sport practiced by the local population at social gatherings and festivals.

This tradition of impromptu and informal competition continued in Arabia and elsewhere until the final three decades of the 20th century, when interested parties began to organize camel racing into a formal sport, similar to that established for Thoroughbred horse

Young boys preparing for a camel race in Dubai, United Arab Emirates. Alain le Garsmeur/Stone

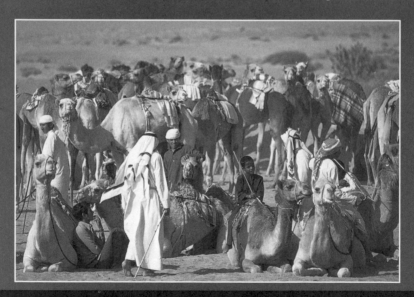

racing. Organizations were established to govern and control camel racing events and to formulate rules and regulations. In countries as diverse as Kenya, the Sudan, Egypt, India, and Australia—but particularly in the Arab countries of the Middle East—the sport became extremely popular, spawning its own training, breeding, and research industries.

Camel racing has come to be recognized as a serious international sport and a great tourist attraction. Events draw participants from throughout the world, and winners of races receive handsome prizes, including large cash awards. Moreover, in those Arab countries that are the sport's core participants, such events reflect the cultural background of the local society. Traditional costumes and rituals are displayed, and the entire day of racing culminates in celebrations that evoke the customs of local peoples. These gatherings help keep local customs and folklore alive, particularly for the younger generation, in a region that is otherwise modernizing rapidly.

THE ARTS

As is true of other countries of the Arabian Peninsula, traditional arts such as pottery, weaving, and metalworking occupy a prominent place in cultural life. The manufacture of handicrafts is an economic mainstay for smaller villages, providing goods to sell in the souks (open-air markets) that lie at the heart of small towns and large cities alike. Traditional storytelling remains a much-admired art form, and Emirati culture, like Arab culture on the whole, esteems poetry, whether it is classical, contemporary, or the Bedouin vernacular form called *nabaṭī*. Traditional music, such as the *ḥudāʾ*—sung originally by caravanners while on the trail—is enjoyed alongside popular music from abroad, and traditional dances such as the *ʿayyālah* (often called *'arḍah*), a type of sword dance, are performed on special occasions.

The Ministry of Information and Culture sponsors a number of events annually, including plays and music festivals, and helps support the numerous folklore associations in the emirates. The Sharjah Theatre Festival brings together talent from all seven emirates. Annual international book fairs in Sharjah and Abu Dhabi cities are highly regarded, and film festivals in the emirates are gaining in popularity and reputation. The Dubai Air Show has become a major regional event.

CULTURAL INSTITUTIONS

Dubai Museum is located in al-Fahīdī Fort and features displays on Bedouin life, local history, dances, and musical instruments. The fort is also home to a military museum. Al-'Ayn is the site of a museum devoted to Bedouin culture and the emirates' pre-oil history. Sharjah city features a noted natural history museum. Dubai city is growing as a centre for regional film, television, and music production.

SPORTS AND RECREATION

Sports are popular in the United Arab Emirates and are strongly supported by the government. The Ministry of Youth and Sports oversees and encourages the many groups, clubs, and associations that provide sports-related activities. Football (soccer) is the most-watched spectator sport, and horse racing also enjoys widespread popularity. The federation is also a major centre for camel racing, a traditional sport that became increasingly popular late in the 20th century, and for falconry, once an important means of hunting. Dubai hosts many international sporting events, most notably for golf, tennis, rugby, and boat racing. The country made its Olympic debut at the 1984 Summer Games.

MEDIA AND PUBLISHING

The news media are concentrated in the emirates of Abu Dhabi, Dubai, and Al-Shāriqah. A number of daily newspapers are published, in both Arabic and English. Radio and television programs are broadcast daily from Abu Dhabi, Dubai, Al-Shāriqah, and Ra's al-Khaymah, in those same languages.

CHAPTER 25

The United Arab Emirates: Past and Present

In the late 18th and early 19th centuries, the dominant tribal faction was the Āl Qawāsim (singular: Qāsimī), whose ships controlled the maritime commerce (notably fishing and pearling) concentrated in the lower Persian Gulf and in much of the Indian Ocean. Attacks on British and Indian ships led to a British naval attack in 1819 that defeated the Qāsimī forces, and the British became dominant in the region.

The Āl Qawāsim thus lost power and influence in the region, and the Banū Yās tribal confederation of Abu Dhabi became dominant. The Banū Yās were centred on the Al-ʿAyn and Al-Liwāʾ oases of Abu Dhabi, and their strength was land-based. Under the leadership of the Āl Nahyān (members of the Āl Bū Falāḥ tribe), the Banū Yās have been the most powerful element in the region since the mid-19th century. The principal sheikhs along the coast signed a series of agreements during that century—a general treaty of peace in 1820, the perpetual maritime truce in 1853 (which gave the Trucial Coast its name), and exclusive agreements in 1892 restricting their foreign relations to British discretion—and the sheikhdoms became known as the Trucial States.

A council of the Trucial States began to meet semiannually in 1952 to discuss administrative issues. In January 1968, following the announcement by the British government that its forces would be withdrawn from the Persian Gulf by late 1971, Trucial Oman and the sheikhdoms of Qatar and Bahrain initiated plans to form a confederation. After three years of negotiations, however, Qatar and Bahrain decided to become independent sovereign states, and the former Trucial States, excluding Raʾs al-Khaymah, announced the formation of the United Arab Emirates in

This photo shows Dubai and its harbour in the 1960s. Paul Popper/Popperfoto/Getty Images

December 1971. Ra's al-Khaymah joined the federation in February 1972.

THE STRUGGLE FOR CENTRALIZATION

Abu Dhabi initiated a movement toward centralization in December 1973, when several of its former cabinet members took positions with the federal government. In May 1976 the seven emirates agreed to merge their armed forces, and in November of that year a provision was added to the constitution that gave the federal government the right to form an army and purchase weapons. Conflicts regarding centralization within the government in 1978 prompted Dubai and Ra's al-Khaymah to refuse to submit their forces to federal command, and Dubai began

Maktūm Dynasty

The Maktūm dynasty (Arabic: Āl Maktūm, "Maktūm family") is the ruling family of the emirate of Dubai of the United Arab Emirates. One of the two members of the Āl Bū Falāsāh family to emigrate from Abu Dhabi to Dubai in 1833 was Baṭī ibn Suhayl, father of Maktūm ibn Baṭī, the first ruler of Dubai (ruled 1833–52). Since that time, the family has played a central role in the leadership of the emirate. The Maktūm are a branch of the same Banū Yās confederation that includes the Āl Nahyān, rulers of Abu Dhabi. In the 1960s members of the Āl Maktūm and Āl Nahyān cooperated to lay the groundwork for self-rule in what would become the United Arab Emirates.

purchasing weapons independently. A proposal to form a federal budget, merge revenues, and eliminate internal boundaries was rejected by Dubai and Ra's al-Khaymah, in spite of strong domestic support. Dubai ended its opposition, however, when its ruler, Sheikh Rāshid ibn Sa'īd al-Maktūm, was offered the premiership of the federal government; he took office in July 1979. Sheikh Zāyid ibn Sulṭān al-Nahyān of Abu Dhabi served as president of the United Arab Emirates from 1971 to his death in 2004, when he was succeeded by his son Sheikh Khalīfah ibn Zāyid al-Nahyān as ruler of Abu Dhabi and president of the emirates. Sheikh Rāshid of Dubai died in 1990, and his positions as ruler of Dubai and vice president and prime minister of the United Arab Emirates were assumed, successively, by his sons Sheikh Maktūm ibn Rāshid al-Maktūm (ruled 1990–2006) and, since 2006, Sheikh Muḥammad ibn Rāshid al-Maktūm.

In 2006 the United Arab Emirates held its first elections. A very limited electoral college was permitted to vote for the selection of half of the membership of the

Nahyān Dynasty

The Nahyān dynasty (Arabic: Āl Nahyān, "Nahyān family") is the ruling family of the emirate of Abu Dhabi, a constituent part of the United Arab Emirates. The family were originally Bedouin of the Banū Yās confederation of Arabia from around the oases of Liwā; in the 1790s they transferred their centre from Liwā to Abu Dhabi. The Nahyān family has long played a leading role in the political life of the emirate. In the 1960s members of the Āl Maktūm and Āl Nahyān cooperated to lay the groundwork for self-rule in what would become the United Arab Emirates, and the country's first president, Sheikh Zāyid ibn Sulṭān, was a member of the Āl Nahyān.

advisory Federal National Council, the other half of which would remain designated by appointment.

FOREIGN RELATIONS

The regime of Ruhollah Khomeini in Iran and the subsequent Iran-Iraq War (1980–88) created problems for the United Arab Emirates. The resurgence of Islamic fundamentalism posed a double threat to the federation's stability by generating unrest among the Iranian Shīʿites living in the emirates and providing inspiration to the growing numbers of young activist Sunnis, who found the existing political order unsupportive and uncommitted to upholding Islamic values.

Fighting during the Iran-Iraq War broke out within a few miles of the emirates' coast when Iran and Iraq began to attack tankers in the Persian Gulf. The intensity of such threats moved the emirates to join with Oman, Qatar, Saudi Arabia, Bahrain, and Kuwait to form the Gulf Cooperation Council (GCC) in 1981. The council was designed to strengthen the security of its members and to promote economic cooperation. The United Arab Emirates joined Saudi Arabia and the other GCC states in condemning Iraq's invasion of Kuwait in 1990. It provided facilities for Western military forces and contributed troops for the liberation of Kuwait in early 1991. The emirates also became a member of both the United Nations and the Arab League in 1991.

The emirates, backed by fellow GCC members, objected vigorously when in 1992 Iran strengthened its control over the disputed islands of Abū Mūsa and the Tunbs (Ṭunb al-Kubrā and Ṭunb al-Ṣughrā), both seized by Iran in 1971. Iran continued to engage in development activities on the islands throughout the decade, including the establishment of an airport on Abū Mūsa and a power station on Ṭunb al-Kubrā in 1996, further straining relations between the two countries; by 2006 no conclusive resolution to these disputes had been reached. The emirates responded by moving closer to the Western powers while maintaining a confrontational stance toward Iran.

In the late 1990s the federation was one of only three countries—along with Pakistan and Saudi Arabia—to recognize the Taliban regime of Afghanistan. The emirates broke relations with that group in 2001, however, when the Taliban refused to extradite Islamic militant Osama bin Laden, accused of organizing the attacks on the World Trade Center in New York City and on the Pentagon outside of Washington, D.C., on September 11.

In early 2006 a fierce debate emerged over the move by state-owned Dubai Ports World (DP World) to take over management of a number of U.S. ports through its acquisition of the British firm that had previously run the ports. Citing security fears, the U.S. Congress threatened to block the deal, which was supported by Pres. George W. Bush. Though political confrontation was averted when DP World committed to divesting of the ports shortly thereafter, the incident provoked strong international debate. In 2007 state-backed Dubai Aerospace Enterprises was also forced to back out of its proposal to purchase a majority stake in the Auckland International Airport in New Zealand; the deal, supported by airport board officials, was faced with overwhelming local council and public opposition.

CONCLUSION

The Arab Persian Gulf states of Bahrain, Kuwait, Oman, Qatar, and the United Arab Emirates share a variety of geographic, economic, cultural, and political features. Geographically, all are arid, and all—with the exception of Oman—are especially small relative to their regional neighbours. In many cases, economic reliance upon petroleum is a persistent issue. Expatriate populations are consistently large, often approaching or surpassing the citizen population. Cultural links and similarities between the countries of the region also remain significant: the primary language in each country is Arabic, with only minor variations in dialect between them. Likewise, all are home to a Muslim majority population, and although Bahrain and Oman are distinct in having a Shīʿite and an Ibāḍī majority, respectively, Kuwait, Qatar, and the United Arab Emirates all have a Sunni majority. In many cases popular political participation is growing; in spite of this, however, rulers—generally drawn from a particular ruling family—remain firmly in control. Social provisions are overall quite good in each country: excellent hospitals, schools, and networks of communication and transport are available in each, and rates of literacy are generally high.

These states are likewise linked by shared historical elements. Due to the location of the region, commercial enterprises have long been important features there, and they remain so. Geopolitical significance has also been an important regional feature: British interests in the region played a substantial role in shaping the gulf states' early modern histories, and, due to the region's powerful neighbours, external security threats have been a regional concern in modern times. This issue was underscored by the Iraqi invasion of Kuwait in 1990, which contributed to the close relationship between some of the countries of the region and the United States. At the beginning of the 21st century, improved security was an important goal; accordingly, military expenditure in the gulf states region is generally high, and military spending in Oman—as a proportion of the country's GDP—is the highest in the world.

The Arab Persian Gulf states of Bahrain, Kuwait, Oman, Qatar, and the United Arab Emirates—once relatively insular and obscure to the West—were in many ways deeply changed by the discovery of oil, and today they boast modern metropolises, advanced infrastructure, and economies of the first order. Through commerce, tourism, education, and the arts, they continue to interact with—and influence—the world at large.

GLOSSARY

alluvial Relating to material, such as soil, that is deposited by running water.

apostate One who renounces or abandons a previous loyalty or faith.

artesian well A well from which water flows under natural pressure without pumping.

Bedouin A nomadic Arab of the Arabian, Syrian, or north African deserts.

caliph A leader who serves as the successor of Muhammad as temporal and spiritual head of Islam.

cistern An artificial reservoir (as an underground tank) for storing liquids and especially water (as rainwater).

civet Any of various Old World carnivorous viverrid mammals with long bodies, short legs, and a usually long tail.

deliberative body A group of persons (such as a jury or legislature) that engages in consideration of and decisions about matters of policy and law.

delimit To fix or define the limits of.

desalinization The removal of dissolved salts from seawater and from the salty waters of inland seas, highly mineralized groundwaters, and municipal wastewaters.

dishdashah A traditional woven cotton robe.

effluent Something, especially a fluid, that flows outward.

emir A ruler, chief, or commander in Islamic countries.

eolian Caused by the wind's action, such as erosion or movement of material from one place to another.

ephemeral Short-lived.

erosion The process of slowly wearing away.

falaj An ancient water channel.

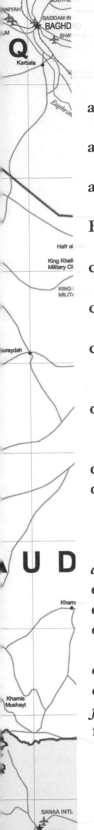

frankincense Aromatic gum resin containing a volatile oil that was valued in ancient times in worship and as a medicine and is still an important incense resin. It is obtained from trees of the genus *Boswellia*. Incisions are made in the trunks of the trees, and the frankincense exudes as a milk-like juice that hardens on exposure to air.

halophytic A plant that grows in salty soil.

hegemony Leadership or predominant influence exercised by one power over another.

hijab A long, flowing headscarf worn by many women in the Islamic world.

jerboa Any of 33 species of long-tailed leaping rodents well adapted to the deserts and steppes of eastern Europe, Asia, and northern Africa. Jerboas are mouse-like, with bodies ranging from 5 to 15 cm (2 to 5.9 inches) in length. All species have short forelegs and extremely long hind legs.

kaffiyeh A headscarf worn by men in the Islamic world, held in place by a cord.

majlis An Islamic council or legislative body.

monsoon A major wind system that seasonally reverses its direction, such as one that blows for approximately six months from the northeast and six months from the southwest.

promulgate To make a doctrine known by open declaration.

sedimentary Formed of or by material deposited by water, wind, or glaciers.

shāwarmah Marinated meat that is grilled or roasted on a spit and served as an entree or on flatbread as a sandwich.

souk A bazaar or open marketplace.

suffrage The right to vote; also the exercise of such a right.

wadi Dry channel or valley in a desert that can be filled with water during the rainy season.

BIBLIOGRAPHY

Comparative coverage of the Persian Gulf states is provided by Helen Chapin Metz (ed.), *Persian Gulf States: Country Studies*, 3rd ed. (1994); John Bulloch, *The Persian Gulf Unveiled* (also published as *The Gulf*, 1984); Alvin J. Cottrell (ed.), *The Persian Gulf States: A General Survey* (1980); Michael Herb, *All in the Family: Absolutism, Revolution, and Democracy in the Middle Eastern Monarchies* (1999); Anthony Cordesman, *Bahrain, Oman, Qatar, and the UAE* (1997); F. Gregory Gause, III, *Oil Monarchies: Domestic and Security Challenges in the Arab Gulf States* (1994); Rosemarie Said Zahlan, *The Making of the Modern Gulf States*, rev. and updated ed. (1998); Khaldoun Hasan al-Naqeeb, *Society and State in the Gulf and Arab Peninsula: A Different Perspective*, trans. from Arabic (1990); Paul Dresch and James Piscatori (eds.), *Monarchies and Nations: Globalisation and Identity in the Arab States of the Gulf* (2005); and Frederick F. Anscombe, *The Ottoman Gulf: The Creation of Kuwait, Saudi Arabia, and Qatar* (1997).

Discussions of early regional history include Juan R.I. Cole, "Rival Empires of Trade and Imami Shi'ism in Eastern Arabia, 1300–1800," *International Journal of Middle East Studies*, 19:177–203 (May 1987); J.B. Kelly, *Britain and the Persian Gulf, 1795–1880* (1968); and Ahmad Mustafa Abu-Hakima, *History of Eastern Arabia, 1750–1800: The Rise and Development of Bahrain and Kuwait* (1965).

Good general accounts of Bahrain include John Whelan (ed.), *Bahrain* (1983); Angela Clarke, *The Islands of Bahrain: An Illustrated Guide to Their Heritage* (1981); and James H.D. Belgrave, *Welcome to Bahrain*, 9th ed. (1975), a detailed guidebook that includes the geography, history, and customs of Bahrain, together with a bibliography of works in Arabic, English, and French. More specific studies of the islands' history include Curtis E. Larsen, *Life and Land Use on the Bahrain Islands: The Geoarcheology of an Ancient Society* (1983); Abbas Faroughy, *The Bahrein Islands, 750–1951: A Contribution to the Study of Power Politics in the Persian Gulf: An Historical, Economic, and Geographical Survey* (1951); and M.G. Rumaihi, *Bahrain: Social and Political Change Since the First World War* (1976). Economic, political, and social conditions are addressed in Jeffrey B. Nugent and Theodore Thomas (eds.), *Bahrain and the Gulf: Past Perspectives and Alternative Futures* (1985), which has a good account of resources and economic development; Fuad I. Khuri, *Tribe and State in Bahrain: The Transformation of Social and Political Authority in an Arab State* (1980); and Mahdi Abdalla Al-Tajir, *Bahrain, 1920–1945: Britain, the Shaikh, and the Administration* (1987). Further bibliographic information can be found in P.T.H. Unwin (compiler), *Bahrain* (1984).

A historical overview of Kuwait is found in Ahmad Mustafa Abu-Hakima, *The Modern History of Kuwait, 1750–1965* (1982). Jill Crystal, *Kuwait: The Transformation of an Oil State* (1992), and *Oil and Politics in the Gulf: Rulers and Merchants in Kuwait and Qatar*, updated ed. (1995); Anthony H. Cordesman, *Kuwait: Recovery and Security After the Gulf War* (1997); and Jacqueline S. Ismael, *Kuwait: Dependency and Class in a Rentier State*, 2nd ed. (1993), examine Kuwait specifically. Mary Ann Tétreault, *The Kuwait Petroleum Corporation and the Economics of the New World Order* (1995), focuses on the oil industry. A thorough study of the ruling family is found in Alan Rush, *Al-Sabah: Genealogy and History of Kuwait's Ruling Family, 1752–1986* (1987). Anh Nga Longva, *Walls Built on Sand: Migration, Exclusion, and Society in Kuwait* (1997); and Shafeeq N. Ghabra, *Palestinians in Kuwait: The Family and the Politics of Survival* (1987), discuss the expatriate population. Comparative studies on border disputes are David H. Finnie, *Shifting Lines in the Sand: Kuwait's Elusive Frontier with Iraq* (1992);

Richard Schofield, *Kuwait and Iraq: Historical Claims and Territorial Disputes*, 2nd ed. rev. and enlarged (1993); and Richard Schofield (ed.), *Territorial Foundations of the Gulf States* (1994).

Works on Oman include Carol J. Riphenburg, *Oman: Political Development in a Changing World* (1998); Miriam Joyce, *The Sultanate of Oman: A Twentieth Century History* (1995); Francis Owtram, *A Modern History of Oman: Formation of the State Since 1920* (2004); Ian Skeet, *Oman: Politics and Development* (1992); Calvin H. Allen, Jr., *Oman: The Modernization of the Sultanate* (1987); Donald Hawley, *Oman & Its Renaissance*, jubilee ed., rev. and reconstructed (1995); B.R. Pridham (ed.), *Oman: Economic, Social, and Strategic Developments* (1987); Liesl Graz, *The Omanis: Sentinels of the Gulf* (1982; originally published in French, 1981); and John Duke Anthony, John Peterson, and Donald Sean Abelson, *Historical and Cultural Dictionary of the Sultanate of Oman and the Emirates of Eastern Arabia* (1976).

Anthropological studies of Oman include Jörg Janzen, *Nomads in the Sultanate of Oman: Tradition and Development in Dhofar* (1986; originally published in German, 1980); and Fredrik Barth, *Sohar: Culture and Society in an Omani Town* (1983). The role of women is the subject of Christine Eickelman, *Women and Community in Oman* (1984), and Unni Wikan, *Behind the Veil in Arabia: Women in Oman* (1982, reissued 1991). Patricia Risso, *Oman & Muscat: An Early Modern History* (1986), is a scholarly treatment of the first half of the 19th century. Oman's relationship with East Africa is covered in M. Reda Bhacker, *Trade and Empire in Muscat and Zanzibar: Roots of British Domination* (1992). John C. Wilkinson, *The Imamate Tradition of Oman* (1987), outlines the background of the events leading to the demise of the Ibāḍī imamate in the 1950s. The challenges facing the state after the 1970 coup d'état are assessed in John Townsend, *Oman: The Making of a Modern State* (1977).

Further information may be found in Frank A. Clements (compiler), *Oman*, rev. and expanded ed. (1994), an annotated bibliography.

A good historical overview of Qatar is found in Rosemarie Said Zahlan, *The Creation of Qatar* (1979). Sources on social conditions include Klaus Ferdinand, *Bedouins of Qatar*, trans. from Danish (1993); and Abeer Abu Saud, *Qatari Women: Past and Present* (1984). Ragaei El Mallakh, *Qatar: Energy and Development* (1985); and Zuhair Ahmed Nafi, *Economic and Social Development in Qatar* (1983), examine economic issues. Nathan J. Brown, *The Rule of Law in the Arab World: Courts in Egypt and the Gulf* (1997), is a study of the judicial system. An analysis of historical and contemporary politics is provided by Jill Crystal, *Oil and Politics in the Gulf: Rulers and Merchants in Kuwait and Qatar*, updated ed. (1995).

Works on the United Arab Emirates include Frank A. Clements (compiler), *United Arab Emirates*, rev. ed. (1998); Werner Forman and Michael Asher, *Phoenix Rising: The United Arab Emirates, Past, Present & Future* (1996); Malcolm C. Peck, *The United Arab Emirates: A Venture in Unity* (1986); and Ali Mohammed Khalifa, *The United Arab Emirates: Unity in Fragmentation* (1979). Linda Usra Soffan, *The Women of the United Arab Emirates* (1980), discusses changes in the status of women. See also Ragaei El Mallakh, *The Economic Development of the United Arab Emirates* (1981).

Historical works include Abdullah Omran Taryam, *The Establishment of the United Arab Emirates, 1950–85* (1987); Sulṭān Muḥammad Al-Qāsimī, *The Myth of Arab Piracy in the Gulf*, 2nd ed. (1988); Muhammad Morsy Abdullah, *The United Arab Emirates: A Modern History* (1978); Rosemarie Said Zahlan, *The Origins of the United Arab Emirates* (1978); Clarence C. Mann, *Abu Dhabi: Birth of an Oil Shaikhdom*, 2nd ed. (1969); and Frauke Heard-Bey, *From Trucial States to United Arab Emirates: A Society in Transition*, new ed. (1996).

INDEX

E

F

G

H

I

R

S

T

U

W

Y